DRINKING  WITH GEORGE

DRINKING WITH GEORGE

A Barstool Professional's
Guide to Beer

GEORGE WENDT

with Jonathan Grotenstein

Simon Spotlight Entertainment
New York   London   Toronto   Sydney

Simon Spotlight Entertainment
A Division of Simon & Schuster, Inc.
1230 Avenue of the Americas
New York, NY 10020

Copyright ©2009 by Padre Productions, Inc.

Photo on page 196 by: NBC Universal Photo Bank.

First Simon Spotlight Entertainment hardcover edition October 2009

SIMON SPOTLIGHT ENTERTAINMENT and colophon are trademarks
of Simon & Schuster, Inc.

For information about special discounts for bulk purchases, please
contact Simon & Schuster Special Sales at 1-866-506-1949 or
business@simonandschuster.com.

The Simon & Schuster Speakers Bureau can bring authors to
your live event. For more information or to book an event
contact the Simon & Schuster Speakers Bureau at 1-866-248-3049
or visit our website at www.simonspeakers.com.

Designed by Jessica Heslin

Manufactured in the United States of America

10   9   8   7   6   5   4   3   2   1

Library of Congress Cataloging-in-Publication Data is available.

ISBN 978-1-4391-4958-4
ISBN 978-1-4391-5815-9 (ebook)

For my family.

CONTENTS

INTRODUCTION

I'm a simple man. I don't ask for much. Give me a nice comfortable chair, a cool breeze, a ball game on the radio, and an
ice-cold beer, and I couldn't be happier.

Truth be told, if it came down to it, I could live without
the chair. A cool breeze is nice, but it isn't exactly manda
tory for a good time. And there are plenty of times when I
don't have access to a ball game.

But a world without beer? I don't know if that's the kind
of world I want to live in.

A lot of people have asked me about my favorite beer. Is
it something with a lot of hoppy character? Something
strong or mild, light or dark, or paired with whatever I'm
eating? It's actually an easy question to answer: yes. Or, put
another way, the idea of picking my favorite beer is like asking me to tell you which of my children I like best. Will Rogers once said he never met a man he didn't like. I feel the
same about beer.

Beer has given a lot over the years: good times, a few great stories, a brain full of useless information, and even a career. Now it's time for me to give something back. So sit down and crack open a cold one—somewhere in the world it's beer o'clock.

Cheers!

DRINKING WITH GEORGE

TO THE
TAVERN BORN

"The key to growth is the introduction of higher
dimensions of consciousness into
our awareness."
—Lao Tzu

 It was customary among Chicago Irish Catholics in the 1950s to use children as beer caddies. Take my wife, Bernadette: When her grandfather's love for storytelling left his throat dry, he sent her out for more beer. She'd step out her back door, walk down an alleyway to the local tavern, and show the bartender a note from her grandfather. That Bernadette was an eleven-year-old with pigtails didn't faze anyone in the slightest—the bartender simply handed her a couple of quarts of beer as if it was milk and sent her on her way.

Running out of beer was never a problem at my house— the fridge was always stocked with cans of Budweiser. "Run along, Bobby," my own grandfather would shout from his favorite chair, "and fetch me a beer."

"Bobby" wasn't the result of too much afternoon drinking—it was actually what people called me through most of my childhood. I was born George Robert Wendt III, which meant my father got to be the George in the family. I'd almost completely forgotten that my name was George until I heard a teacher calling it out on my first day of kindergarten. "I guess that's me," I finally replied. I like to think this kind of flexibility prepared me for later in life, when complete strangers started calling me "Norm."

After I'd retrieved the beer for my grandfather—and opened the can with a church key—I got my reward: a taste. I'll never forget the first time he let me try his beer, when I was maybe eight years old. Since then I've tossed back plenty of brews that are supposed to be better than Bud, but nothing's ever going to match that first sip. For some people, beer's an acquired taste. Not me. Right off the bat I thought I was drinking a little bit of heaven—no mystery as to how the church key got its name.

Nowadays our grandparents would probably be accused of enabling alcoholism. But I've always suspected that babies are born loving beer. Bernadette's grandfather taught her twin brothers to walk by holding out a beer can. Maybe it's a regional thing: French babies might love wine, while Russian rugrats enter the world with a taste for vodka. I wouldn't know—in Chicago, beer is pretty much synonymous with mother's milk.

I was definitely born loving beer.

· · ·

There have been breweries in Chicago since the 1830s, when "Chicago" meant a few hundred settlers surrounded by corn and wigwams full of pissed-off Potawatomis. The settlement was eventually invaded, not by angry Native Americans but European immigrants, mostly German and Irish. The Germans brought lager and a drinking culture that stretched back centuries. The Irish brought their thirst. I'm either fortunate or cursed to have been born into both heritages.

My father's people were actually from Danzig, which is the same place that Poland calls Gdansk. It's been part of Poland for over a thousand years, except for the almost two hundred years it was part of Germany. So while my father's people called themselves Germans, I'm still on the fence as to whether or not I should be offended by Polish jokes.

Not that there was a lot of talk about the Old Country in my home—all four of my grandparents were born in Chicago, or County Cook, in the vernacular of the South Side Irish. As a kid, the only thing I knew about my mother's people was that they were from Ireland. Years later, while planning a visit to her ancestral land, I asked her exactly where.

"Oh," she said, "Mayo, God help us."

"Oh," I said. "You mean County Mayo?"

"Maybe," she admitted. "I've just never heard it said without the 'God help us.' "

A PROPER PINT

There are plenty of fine beers brewed in Ireland: Beamish, Harp, Kilkenny, Murphy's, and Smithwick's, to name a few. But when an Irishman (or woman) refers to "a proper pint," they're probably talking about Guinness. And the only way to appreciate a Guinness is to drink one pulled from the tap.

Unless you happen to live in Dublin, however, you're not going to find a proper pint. You may *think* you're drinking the real Guinness, but in the eyes of many Irish beer snobs, their sacred stout loses quality the farther away you get from the old brewery at St. James's Gate.

My first visit to Ireland was a short one—an overnight trip to Belfast for an appearance on a local chat show. I made only one request of the show's producers: I had to have a proper pint of Guinness. "No problem," they assured me. "We'll take you out after the show."

We wrapped around eleven P.M., which also happens to be closing time for most Irish pubs, but the producers promised me that they knew a place that was open. We entered a bar that didn't look anything like the Irish pub in my mind's eye—instead, a Liberace-clone played piano to screaming old ladies—but I wasn't about to let the aesthetics interfere with my single-minded goal. "A pint of Guinness, please."

The bartender raised his hands apologetically. "We don't carry Guinness here."

"All right," I conceded. "How about a Murphy's?" No. "Harp?" No. I worked my way through every Irish beer I knew. The bartender just shook his head each time. "So what do you have?" I finally asked.

"Bud, Bud Light, Coors, Coors Light . . ."

Now don't get me wrong, I'll happily drink any of those beers at an All-American picnic or a barbecue, preferably from a tub filled with ice. But not on my first trip to Ireland. Fortunately, a helpful waiter noticed my frustration. "I might be able to get you a Guinness," he volunteered, sprinting across the street to a closing pub and returning with a couple of freshly poured glasses of the good stuff.

It was delicious, so much so that I later bragged about the experience to some of my Irish friends. They weren't exactly impressed. "In Belfast, you say? That's not a proper pint."

It wouldn't have mattered if I was in Kilkenny, Limerick, or Cork—I had to be in Dublin to drink a real Guinness. I wouldn't find a reason to visit Dublin for several years, but when I did, I went straight for the teat, pulling a draft off a keg inside the brewery's company store. I also bought a postcard for my Irish friends, inscribing it with the words "This proper enough for you?"

‖‖

I got drunk for the first time when I was sixteen, at the 1965 World's Fair in New York City, where I was visiting my sister, a hostess at the Illinois pavilion. During the day, the Fair was a testament to "Man's Achievement on a Shrinking Globe in an Expanding Universe" and included the premiere of an animatronic Disney show called "It's a Small World." After midnight, once the mostly teenage staff was rid of the guests, the Fair became an international kegger. Party at the French pavilion! Party at the Japanese pavilion! I remember making a fool out of myself trying (unsuccessfully) to vault a hitching post at the Texas pavilion. Fortunately, my idiotic behavior escaped the notice of one of the other hostesses at the Illinois pavilion—my future wife, Bernadette. Small world, indeed.

I brought my taste for beer back home with me. But for Catholic teenagers in 1960s Chicago like me, with zero interest in politics or activism, there weren't exactly a lot of opportunities to get wild and crazy. I spent the rest of the summer hanging out at Janson's, a drive-in at 99th and Western. It was a lot like *American Graffiti,* except instead of souped-up hot rods, the kids drove their parents' Plymouths.

One day my friend Terry Thulis and I got restless and wandered up the block to 100th Street, where we stumbled across a bar called Littleton's. It was your standard neighborhood "old man" bar, dark and musty. Neither of us looked like old men: I was your typical sixteen-year-old kid, while Terry, a late bloomer, couldn't have looked older than nine. But that didn't stop us from dreaming. "Maybe they'll serve us," I said.

We poked our heads inside. It was dark. Very dark. *Bizarrely* dark. As our eyes adjusted, we saw that the place was nearly empty except for a couple of grizzled drunks at the bar. I nudged Terry. "Should we?"

We tried to look casual as we strode to the bar. The bartender was an older guy, maybe seventy, with white hair and eyes set so deep that you could hardly see them. He hummed a happy tune as he stacked some glasses, and he greeted us warmly when he noticed we were there. "Oh, hello!"

"We'd like a couple of drafts," I said, hoping my voice wouldn't crack.

"Coming right up!"

A few seconds later, he deposited a pair of beers in front of us. I looked at Terry in stunned disbelief. We emptied our glasses as fast as we could . . . and asked for two more.

"Sure thing!" the bartender replied. Chipper fellow. But there was something weird about his eyes. . . .

"George," Terry said, nudging me under the bar. "I think he's blind." He waved his hand toward the bartender. No reaction. I did the same. Still no reaction.

"I think you're right!" I said. I looked over at the two drunks at the bar, who clearly weren't blind. They were shaking their heads in disgust, universal sign language for "you little motherfuckers."

"So wait a minute," Terry whispered. "We have just found a bar, one block away from Janson's, with a blind bartender who will serve us beer?"

"We can't tell *anyone*," I whispered back. "Not a word!" We quickly made a pact to keep our newfound oasis a secret.

Our "secret" lasted about fifteen minutes. By the following week, Littleton's was overflowing with what used to be the Janson's crowd: dozens of bicycles parked in front, a hundred rowdy teenagers inside. My guess is that the two old drunks tipped off the cops, who showed up that weekend to bust up the party.

LOUDMOUTH SOUP

Everyone knows that beer is a social lubricant, but even scientists have trouble explaining why. The most popular theory is that alcohol affects the amygdala—the brain's pleasure center—producing extra gamma-aminobutyric acid, or GABA, which makes us feel happy and reduces stress. So now you know: It's GABA that creates the gift of gab.

While the loss of Littleton's was definitely a bummer, Terry and I weren't going to let it get in the way of our quest for beer. We heard a story about a neighborhood bar in South Shore that might be amenable to serving the age-impaired, so we hopped on a bus and headed on over. Jackpot! Not only did the old men inside ignore our peach fuzz, but the drafts were just fifteen cents a pop. At that price we could drink like kings. Which we did.

Unlike kings, we had no royal coach to take us home. By the time the bar closed the buses had stopped running for the night, and we'd drank away our cab fare hours before. And since we were engaging in illegal behavior, we couldn't exactly call our parents to come pick us up.

Fortunately, we had a time-honored tradition at our disposal: fare ditching. We called a cab, and while we waited for it to arrive, we concocted a plan. There was a stop sign at 91st and Leavitt. When the cab came to a halt, we'd jump out of the back and escape down some nearby alleyways. As long as we remained inconspicuous until the last possible minute, the driver wouldn't suspect a thing.

We got into the cab and gave the driver a fake address, one that would take us through 91st and Leavitt. When we stopped at the intersection, Terry leapt out and sprinted for the alleyways. He was well on his way to freedom when he realized that he didn't hear my footsteps behind him.

I'd passed out drunk in the back of the cab.

By the time Terry came back to look for me, the driver was shaking me against the side of the car. I was too terrified to do anything except blurt out my real address. I'll never forget the way my mother shook her head at me as she settled our fare. Thank God she never told my father.

The Birth of Beer

The oldest recipe known to man is a 4,000-year-old clay tablet inscribed by ancient Mesopotamians. When archaeologists deciphered its runes, they discovered instructions— apparently passed down from the God of Water himself, the mighty Enki—for brewing beer.

The Mesopotamians weren't the only ones with the secret recipe. The Chinese brewed beer out of millet, while across the drink, Incans fermented corn into their own version of South American sunshine. Beer may very well be a gift from the gods, but the recipe was probably discovered by people, probably by accident.

Imagine Ooog, a caveman living in 10,000 B.C. who liked to plan ahead. While most of his friends waited until they were hungry before embarking on the hunt or foraging for nuts and berries, Ooog collected wild barley and brought it back to his cave, where Mrs. Ooog could whip up a meal whenever the kids' stomachs started to grumble. Given that not even cave-kids liked to eat vegetables, she probably mashed it up with some water to make a sort of gruel.

Ooog is prepared, but forgetful. One day he forgets to close the rock in front of the cave and rain gets in, soaking the grains. He puts them out in the sun, hoping they'll dry before Mrs. Ooog gets wise. Or maybe the kids notice that a few of the grains in their gruel have sprouted, making them taste a little sweeter than the rest, and Mrs. Ooog sets them aside for dessert. Either way, the germinating grains are allowed to dry out, inadvertently triggering a process called *malting*.

The Ooogs don't know anything about the invisible wild yeast floating around in their cave. But the yeast sniffs out the malted grains, transforming them into a dark, bubbly liquid that smells kind of funny. "Better throw this away," says Mrs. Ooog.

"Are you kidding me? It's perfectly edible," replies Ooog, drinking some of the liquid to prove his point. He braces himself for the bad taste, only to find out he doesn't have to—he likes it. *Really* likes it, despite a headache the next day. He starts to tell his friends about this new delicacy. The Ooogs' cave quickly becomes a popular destination, with Mrs. Ooog dishing out the stuff by the bowlful.

AN IRISH
EDUCATION

"Instead of giving money to found colleges to
promote learning, why don't they pass a
constitutional amendment prohibiting anybody
from learning anything? If it works as good
as the Prohibition one did, why, in five years
we would have the smartest race of
people on earth."
—Will Rogers

 I always knew that I was going to go to Notre
Dame. My father, Class of '43, started taking me to
Fighting Irish football games when I was just a
little kid. Every Saturday we'd drive to the Land
O' Lakes Gun Club in La Porte, Indiana, where
we'd eat a catered sit-down lunch before riding to
South Bend on a chartered bus. Afterward the bus would

13

take us back to the clubhouse, where we'd eat hot dogs and chili before driving back to Chicago.

These meals were attended by doctors, lawyers, bankers—professionals who wore a suit and tie even on Saturday. They had two things in common: degrees from Notre Dame and a love of drink. My father and his contemporaries were America's greatest cocktail generation, tossing back highballs and martinis like they were water. But while the drinking occasionally bordered on immodest, it was never irresponsible. There was no way, for example, that anyone was going to serve alcohol to a kid like me.

As I got older, I realized my opportunity was in the walk from the parking lot to the football stadium. I'd let my father get a head start, then I'd lag behind to mingle with the tailgaters. My first hangover came after one of these walks, thanks to Gluek Stite, a beer so exotic, so strong, that I was sure it was an import. It wasn't until I started to write this book that I found out Gluek Stite was what today we'd call a malt liquor from Minnesota.

STRONG BEER

Most beers wind up with an alcohol content of about 5 percent once the natural brewing process is complete. Some brewers have figured out how to reduce this number, creating near beer (useful for alcoholics and the liver-impaired) and that dreaded con-

14

cession to sobriety, "three-two," named for its 3.2 percent alcohol content (I'm looking at you, Utah).

A few hardy souls have taken the fight in the other direction, pursuing higher levels of alcohol content. For years, that meant malt liquor, a beverage that is to beer what crack cocaine cut with baby laxatives is to the finest Peruvian flake. But today we live in a golden age of beer, where skilled brewers make amazing craft brews with three times the wallop of a Colt 45. Ladies and gentlemen, I bring you the strongest beers in the world:

Schorschbräu Eisbock (30.86 percent alcohol by volume)
Südstern XXL (27.6 percent alcohol by volume)

It shouldn't come as any surprise that the world's most überbeers are from Germany. Both of these beers are crafted Eisbock-style: The brewers freeze the beer and scrape off the ice, eliminating a portion of the water content. What's left is a beer that is more concentrated—and therefore more alcoholic. Some purists think this is cheating, but man, what a wallop!

Samuel Adams Utopias (27 percent alcohol by volume)
America's contribution to hops-induced degeneracy. I think it's tastier than the Eisbocks, but it goes down more like a cognac than a beer.

Struise Double Black (26 percent alcohol by volume)
Belgium may not have had much luck with the Germans in wartime, but when it comes to beers, the Belgians have been up to

the task for centuries. This beer is also brewed Eisbock-style
but begins its life as an Imperial stout—think Samuel Smith on
steroids!

⁂

But before I could get to Notre Dame, I had to survive Campion Jesuit, an all-boys boarding prep school in Wisconsin that operated like a prison camp. Anyone who showed free will, chutzpah, or the slightest sign of actually owning a set of balls was quickly weeded out: Of the 180 kids in my freshman class, maybe a hundred were still around for graduation. We were kept in line by the fear of JUG—Justice Under God, which is what the Jesuits called demerits. Talking in class? Two JUGs. Forget to put the cap back on the toothpaste? Two JUGs. I once got two JUGs for "running" down the hallway, despite the fact that I was on crutches, thanks to a broken foot. The thought of drinking beer never crossed my mind—the consequences of getting caught were too terrifying to imagine.

On top of the fear of dismissal and the occasional threat of corporal punishment, there was mandatory Junior ROTC training. Every Saturday morning, we had to put on army uniforms that never fit quite right and march around campus with dummy M-1 rifles. Once a year, the uniforms would stay on through Saturday night, when we'd be treated to a military ball, a dance with a nearby girls' school. The student officers got to wear full military dress uniform, which included a ceremonial saber. Whoever decided to arm a group of teenagers with military swords clearly hadn't thought things all the way through. It took all of thirty seconds for my friend Joe Keenan to get into an actual duel before the dance even started, taking a slash to the hand that required stitches. Amazingly, he avoided any disciplinary measures for the fight. But he was still dinged two JUGs for showing up late to the dance.

It was the kind of environment that molded politicians, generals, even heads of state. Not so much for me. I was a solid C-student whose October birthday meant I was one of the youngest (read: immature) kids in my class. At the start of my senior year, Father Doran—a Jesuit priest and Campion's principal—called me into his office. "Tell me, George," he said from across his desk. "Do you know where you'll be going to school next year?"

"Oh yes, Father. I'm going to Notre Dame." Nothing was going to keep me away from those tailgates.

Father Doran went silent for what must have been a full minute; clearly, he didn't share my optimism. "Have you ever considered Rockhurst College?" he finally asked.

"Rockhurst? Uh, no. That's in Kansas City, right? No offense, Father, but I'm pretty set on Notre Dame."

Father Doran rolled his eyes, sighed, and wished me luck.

Fortunately, I didn't need luck. One upside of Jesuit prep school was the heavy exposure to Latin—extremely helpful for figuring out root words on standardized tests. I wouldn't say I aced the SATs, but I did better than my grades would have predicted. More important, my father made me a legacy, sort of like the Bushes at Yale. I started Notre Dame as a seventeen-year-old in the fall of 1966.

Father Doran's concerns turned out to be mostly unfounded: Notre Dame's academic curriculum wasn't beyond me. Or, I should say, *wouldn't* have been had I gone to class or done any work at all. But after Campion's rules and restrictions, Notre Dame was like Sodom and Gomorrah. The first night I was there, I hitchhiked with another freshman from Chicago whom I'd just met, Mike McDonald, to a bar in Niles, Michigan, where we stayed up into the wee hours drinking beer. The conversation was heavy: God, war, and serious stuff. Mike and I had both grown up in Irish Catholic families that weren't big fans of intimate or meaningful conversations, especially when the kids were around. The beer helped us cut through the bullshit, or so we thought, getting right to the heart of things. You know, like, "Life . . . Wow . . ."

Hitchhiking back from Niles, Michigan, at three A.M. proved to be a challenge. By the time we got back to campus, my new roommates were already awake, brushing their teeth, and preparing for the first day of orientation. I climbed into bed and slept all day. Orientation, schmorientation. I'd already forged two key college relationships: with Mike and with beer.

THE GAS CREDIT CARD:
A CLASSIC COLLEGE CON

Falling in love with beer was easy. Figuring out how to pay for it was the hard part. Fortunately, my father had given me everything I needed in the form of a gas station credit card. Not that he knew about the gift: I'd lifted the card out of his desk drawer before heading off to college.

Nowadays this hardly seems like a trick—a lot of gas stations sell beer. Back then it meant volunteering—nay, *insisting*—on paying for every tank of gas every time we took a road trip. Then I'd recoup as much hard cash as I could from the driver and passengers, which could in turn be converted directly into beer. I could even afford to give my friends a slight discount, given that the credit card statements went directly to my dad.

My father wasn't an idiot. He once pointed out, after looking over one of the bills, that I could have driven to the moon and back for all the mileage I seemed to be racking up. "Isn't that what college is all about?" I asked him. "Broadening one's horizons?"

"Broadening one's belt, more like it."

Mike McDonald quickly became my partner in crime, along with Joe Keenan and a couple of buddies from high school who'd also ended up at Notre Dame. On Friday afternoons, we'd walk or hitchhike down to a bar near campus that served quarts of Stroh's for fifty-five cents. After four or five quarts, we'd stagger back to campus—rare was the driver amenable to picking up seven or eight drunken freshmen—where we'd make fun of the Notre Dame marching band as they crossed the quad on their way to the Friday evening pep rally.

If all this sounds, well, a little lame, it was: Notre Dame didn't go coed until the 1970s. We were so desperate to meet women that we used to linger right outside campus and pretend to be hitchhikers whenever we saw a car full of potentially eligible ladies. You can probably guess how well that went. Our only other resource was the occasional off-campus house party, which might attract girls from town or one of the local women's colleges. A woman at a Notre Dame house party must have felt like a steak dangled in front of starving wolves.

At one such party, Mike and I honed in on a couple of ladies standing near the bar. So had everyone else, including several members of a local gang. Yes, Notre Dame had its own gang. They called themselves the Black Hand, and the members were from Pittsburgh, a place none of us had ever been, but at least it sounded tough enough to spawn a gang. The pinnacle of the Black Hand's success (if sin can be described as "success" at a Catholic university) was a heist: They robbed the campus bookstore, which sounds pretty tame until you stop to consider that at the time, at least on Saturdays during football season, the Notre Dame bookstore was the busiest retail outlet in the world.

None of that was on our minds as we tried to chat up a

couple of young ladies at a party. When one of the gang members asked us to back off, Mike responded as he usually did after he'd had a few beers, which means like a smart ass. "Why?" he asked. "Are you going to fight me?"

Actually? Yes. A bunch of the gang members surrounded him. Mike may have been a drunken smart ass, but he was also pre-med and had a clear grip on the threat of bodily harm. He sprinted outside to a friend's car and jumped in. When a member of the Black Hand flashed brass knuckles at the window, the driver stepped on the gas and drove away.

Without me.

I chased after the car as fast as I could. After a block or so, I realized I wasn't alone—the entire gang was chasing after him, demanding blood. Some instinct for self-preservation told me that this was a good time to try and blend in. I stopped yelling "Mike, wait up!" and started yelling "We're going to get you, you bastard!" and "Get ready to die, ass-hole!"

The ploy worked for a couple of blocks, until the car disappeared into the distance. "Damn, he got away!" I said.

"Who the hell are you?" one of the gang members finally thought to ask.

I dodged. I feinted. If Notre Dame's football coach Ara Parseghian had seen me, I might have earned a scholarship on the spot. I took a couple of blows to the head but managed to avoid serious harm long enough to flag down a passing car, some Good Samaritan who dropped me off on campus.

I DEDICATE THIS DRINK
TO CARDINAL PUFF . . .

Drinking games have always struck me as a bit superfluous. Like I really need to trick myself into drinking more beer. But at college, we played them all: Anchorman, Quarters, Speed Quarters, Asshole, Mexican, Thumper, you name it. We went to a Catholic school, so the game we played most often was the appropriately themed Cardinal Puff.

Everyone starts with a full bottle of beer, although mugs or glasses work just as well. The game begins when the first player says "I dedicate the first drink of the night to Cardinal Puff," then taps the top of the table once with both index fingers, does the same to the bottom of the table, snaps with both hands, lifts the beer with his or her index finger and thumb, hits the table one time with the bottle, taps the bottle in the air, and takes a big swig.

Got that? You'd better: If you mess up, you've got to finish your entire beer and start with a new one. Round One ends when everyone has successfully accomplished the routine or is too drunk to continue. Then it's on to Round Two, which is just like Round One, except that you say "I dedicate the *second* drink of the night to Cardinal Puff," and all of the tapping, snapping, and pounding gets done two times instead of one. In Round Three, you do everything three times. After the third and final swig, you turn the bottle upside down over your head and declare "Once a Cardinal, always a Cardinal. . . . Drink to the last drop!" If there's any beer left in your bottle—or, now, in your hair—you've got to start the whole game over again.

Just one of the many merits of a Catholic education.

‖‖

Despite my lack of interest in anything academic, I managed to squeak by for as long as I lived on campus. (A note of apology to the dormitory residents of 30 Pangborn: That stain inside the dresser drawer isn't coffee.) But my junior year, I moved off-campus with Joe Keenan and a couple of other guys into the second floor of a former firehouse. We had a very good relationship with Mary Mellow, who ran the antique shop underneath us, in that her store was closed during prime partying hours, and we never complained about the noise she and her customers made during the day.

The church across the street was an entirely different matter, with its morning bells at seven A.M. You'd think the sound would have reminded me to get to class; instead, I just burrowed my head into the pillow and went back to sleep. The Angelus bell at noon let me know it was time to wake up.

‖‖‖

While not much of what I learned at Notre Dame has stuck with me over the years, I still use the idea "I would rather sleep than . . ." to evaluate most of the major (and pretty much all of the minor) decisions in my life. If I'd rather be sleeping, say, than waking up at the crack of dawn to play golf or go fishing, then you can bet I'm not going to be golfing or fishing.

|||||||||||||||||||||||||||||||||||||||||||||||||||||||||||||||||||||||||||||||||||||||||||||||||||||||||||||||||||||||||||||||||||||||||||||||||||||||||||||||

Living off-campus didn't cause my grades to slip but to completely disappear. The last straw was a spontaneous decision to go to a party on a weeknight—in Denver, a thousand miles away from any classroom, where some friends of mine from Campion were attending Regis College. It took us eighteen hours to get there in a tiny MG convertible—no backseat, so I was jammed sideways in the boot—and no one was in any hurry to repeat the trip the next day. We decided to keep partying instead. When we finally got back to South Bend, about a week later, I'd ensured a perfect semester: a 0.0 G.P.A. unblemished by even the smallest speck of academic achievement. I didn't bother with finals—I didn't even know when or where they were. Back at home during winter break, I received a telegram, news far too urgent for the U.S. mail: I was no longer welcome at Notre Dame. The tone of the letter made me think there'd be trouble if I even tried to re-enter Indiana.

I probably would have drifted aimlessly for a while if not for the fear of military conscription. College was the only thing standing between me and the escalating war in Vietnam. The only place that would take me on such short notice, especially with my grades, was Chicago's Roosevelt University.

. . .

Roosevelt was a time of personal discovery, specifically the discovery of girls, Jews, and hippies. It was a blast. At the time, however, it was still a commuter school, meaning I had to live at home. Not good, especially with my dad breathing fire over my expulsion from his alma mater—bye-bye, social life. If I was ever going to drink another beer, I was going to need a college campus.

Fortunately, salvation came in the form of Father Frank Carey. He'd been the director of admissions at Campion Jesuit; now he served in the same capacity at Rockhurst College in Kansas City, the school I'd pooh-poohed to Father Doran. Neither Father Carey nor Rockhurst was in the habit of accepting rejects, but in my case they were willing to make an exception.

That didn't mean I was going to get special treatment once I was there. After I skipped a few lectures early into my Rockhurst career, I found myself back in an administration office. This time the priest told me that if I missed one more class I was through. No excuses. "What if I'm sick?" Nope. "Death in the family?" Sorry, but no.

So for the first time in my college career, I started going to class on a regular basis, even experimenting with homework. School was suddenly a whole lot easier. While some of the older students lived off-campus, I stuck to the dorms. I managed to graduate with a B.A. in economics.

Every once in a while I go back to one of my old schools

This was taken at my high school graduation. Maybe someday I'll actually get my degree from Notre Dame.

to give a speech at a pep rally or fundraiser: Rockhurst out of gratitude; Notre Dame because I'm angling for an honorary degree, still hoping to please my now-departed dad. But my angle—"Do you really want Regis Philbin to be the 'Notre Dame Guy'?"—hasn't paid off for me yet. Neither has my standard stump speech. "There's a rumor that I was kicked out for pulling a 0.0 during my junior year," I always begin. "But nothing could be farther from the truth. I was actually advised by Coach Ara Parseghian that I'd taken drinking on a barstool as far as I could on an amateur basis. It was time for me to turn pro."

The line usually gets a laugh, but the truth is that aside from the Coach Parseghian reference, I'm not really joking. After college I was ready to take my beer drinking to the next level. And that meant Europe.

EUROPEAN VACATIONS

"A fine beer may be judged with only one sip,
but it's better to be thoroughly sure."
—Old Czech proverb

 One thing I did learn in college, or at least during a summer home from college, was that beer didn't have to be yellow or American. A friend of mine took me to a bar on the South Side—the Import Tap, on 51st and Western—where we thought we could get served. As the name might suggest, imports were the house specialty. That was the night I tasted Würzburger Hofbräu. On tap. Man, did the Europeans know how to make beer. A whole new world opened up for me, just one that was cruelly way too expensive to visit very often.

A couple of years later, during my spring break at Rockhurst, we took a family trip to Europe: your typical ten cities in fourteen days—not enough time for any one of them to stand out. Except for Munich, Germany, where the Hofbräuhaus am Platzl blew my little mind.

If you're a committed beer drinker, the Hofbräuhaus might be your kind of paradise. From the outside it looks like your average four-hundred-year-old inn. But the inside is way too loud for anyone to sleep. The front of the building is a giant room, with ceilings maybe fifty feet high, lined with medieval flags. Hundreds of people are seated at long communal tables, many of them locals: Bavarian men in suspenders and lederhosen wearing funny green hats with feathers. More Bavarian men with trumpets, trombones, and accordions play live music, songs that are probably as old as the inn. One particular tune quickly became my favorite: "Oans, zwoa, g'suffa," which a cheerful fellow drinker translated for me as "One, two, chug!" Which we did, gulping the *haus* brew out of liter mugs. No one's glass stayed empty for long, thanks to hearty überwaitresses dressed like the St. Pauli Girl who ferried a dozen mugs at a time. The back of the building was, conveniently enough, a brewery. Not just any brewery but the royal brewery, from back when Germany had kings. One member of my family—who shall remain nameless—got into a drinking contest with a local named Bruno. The next morning, my father had to settle up with the hotel on account of a set of urine-soaked sheets. (I swear to you, it wasn't me.)

III

BEER ME!

IIIIIIIIIIIIIIIIIIIIIIIIIIIIIIIIIIIIIIIIIIIIIIIIIIIIIIIIIIIIIIIIIIIIIIIIIIIIIIIIIIIIIIIIIIIIIIIIIIIIIIIIIIIIIIIIIIIIIIIIIIIIIIIII

One of the defining characteristics of the Hofbräuhaus are the waitresses carrying what look like a dozen beer steins at once, each mug weighted by a liter of beer, barely spilling a drop. A barmaid in Munich named Anita Schwartz set the modern-day standard for excellence, carrying sixteen steins for forty meters without spilling. But in 2007 Reinhard Wurtz, owner of a German-style beer hall in Sydney, Australia, set out to break her record, carrying twenty-one steins through a forty-meter obstacle course. He dropped one, but let's give the man some credit: Twenty's still pretty impressive.

Ms. Schwartz tried to break the record in 2008, setting out with twenty-one steins arranged in a pyramid, but the formation collapsed—two beers tragically spilled to the ground. Still, to honor her achievement, *The Guinness Book of World Records* decided that her nineteen-beer carry was worth its own mention as "Most Beer Steins Carried Over Forty Meters—Female."

IIIIIIIIIIIIIIIIIIIIIIIIIIIIIIIIIIIIIIIIIIIIIIIIIIIIIIIIIIIIIIIIIIIIIIIIIIIIIIIIIIIIIIIIIIIIIIIIIIIIIIIIIIIIIIIIIIIIIIIIIIIIIIIII

I returned home from Europe and soon embarked on what I figured would be my real life. I finally graduated from Rockhurst, not with exceptional grades, but at least with a degree. My dad gave me a job—as a gofer in his real estate office—and I started thinking about what I wanted to do with the rest of my days. About three minutes later, I realized I didn't have a clue. So I asked my friend Mike McDonald for advice.

While I'd been partying myself into oblivion at Notre Dame, I'd always assumed that Mike was doing the same. Man, was I wrong: He was secretly acing his classes, graduating in three years and preparing himself for medical school. (Today my old drinking buddy is an ear, nose, and throat surgeon.) Clearly, he had his shit far better put together than I did.

"What you do," Mike said, "is you go back to Europe."

In the early '70s, "Europe" was a code word for "bohemian life-style." While I considered myself too cool to be a hippie—I thought I was too cool to be anything—I appreciated their emphasis on rock and roll, free love, and the occasional toke from a peace pipe. You could still visit Europe cheaply back then, when guidebooks promised to show you how to do it on five dollars a day. After investing $165 in a round-trip ticket to Luxembourg, I did it on about five cents, sleeping in a tent by the side of the road. I carried only a small backpack, mostly filled with a suit and good shoes that my father insisted I take with me. ("You won't get in anyplace without a suit and good shoes," he said.)

In Rome, I was accosted by an American with long hair and a beard that made him look like Buffalo Bill. "I don't have any money," I quickly told him.

"George, it's me!" he replied. "Begley. I used to work at Nicola's!" I squinted hard, struggling to imagine him with-

It's no wonder it took over a month to get to Morocco.

out the facial hair, until it clicked. Nicola's was one of my favorite haunts from my Notre Dame days, a tavern about a mile from campus. Begley had very often been the guy tending the bar.

"Begley! Great to see you, man! What are you up to?"

"We got a van and we're looking for riders. We're headed to Morocco the slow way. Wanna come?"

ROME TO MOROCCO: THE SLOW WAY

1. Wake up in tent. Look at map. Set ambitious goal for the day's driving.

2. Pile into van. Find nearest village or town with a café. Sip coffee. Read three-day-old *International Herald Tribune*. Get eyeballed suspiciously by locals.

3. Look at watch. Decide it's late enough in the day for one road beer. Play foosball with local kids. Lose badly.

4. Admit to the locals that you're from Chicago. "Ah, Chicago! Al Capone! *Rat-a-tat-a-tat!* Let us buy you a beer!" Decide that, hey, one more beer couldn't hurt.

5. Greet local geezer who lived in Chicago for thirty years before retiring to the Old Country. Toast to the old days. Order another round.

6. Stare at the table full of empty bottles. Wonder where the day went.

7. Stagger into van. Drive to nearest potential campsite. Total distance covered: approximately 2.3 kilometers.

8. Pitch tent. Pass out. Repeat Step 1.

Over a month later, we arrived in Morocco. Caesar's legions had probably made better time from Rome on foot than we did in the van. We made somewhat better time to Portugal, where one of the riders—Dick Rolston, an Iowa boy fresh out of the navy—introduced us to Lisbon's notorious sailor bars. They were gnarly, debauched joints where NATO seamen mingled with whores and pirates.

We decided to stay for a while.

Looking to lighten my load, I packed a leather travel bag I'd overpaid for in Marrakesh with my untouched and completely unnecessary suit and dress shoes. I sent them back to the States via tramp steamer, addressing the bag to my friend Joe Farmar so as not to offend my dad. A few months later, I would try to recover the clothes, only to discover that Joe had torn the suit, the shoes, and even the bag itself to shreds. This was entirely my fault: I hadn't bothered to include a note, which confused Joe until he put "bag" together with "Marrakesh" and decided that I'd hidden hashish somewhere inside.

I finally returned to Chicago in the fall, replenished my funds working for my dad, and went right back to Europe the following February. This time I was prepared: Joe Keenan, Dick Rolston, and I went in together on a VW van. The plan was for Dick and me to pick up the van in Hanover, Germany, then drive south to Spain where we'd meet up with Joe and another friend.

There were a few twists and turns along the way. Hours after arriving in Luxembourg, Dick and I managed to lose most of our bankroll to an unscrupulous hash dealer. (Don't ask.) We got some better news when we picked up the van in Hanover: Apparently we were eligible to receive a cash rebate—in six weeks. Fortunately, two of my sisters were in Rome on a year-abroad study program. I gave the VW dealer their address, drove to Spain to pick up the rest of our party, then traveled to Rome, where I spent the next month pretending to be a student at the school my sisters were attending, sleeping in the dorm and eating in the cafeteria with the rest of my "classmates." I became so familiar to the students and faculty that I considered running for student council. The check finally arrived, but we lost Dick, who had embarked on a torrid affair with an Italian woman. After a brief detour to Greece, Joe and I made our way to Germany: I'd been plotting a return to the Hofbräuhaus all summer.

In those days, before ATMs were everywhere and everyone had credit cards, American tourists never left home without their traveler's checks. The theory was that they were safe, supposedly theftproof: You needed to double-sign the checks in order to use them, which clearly was above petty criminals' capabilities. Our problem was that none of the local merchants wanted to take them. We were getting murdered on the exchange rate, until we stumbled upon the idea of going to a bank and exchanging our American traveler's checks for the German version. Problem solved. Or so we thought.

We went straight from the bank to the Hofbräuhaus,

where Joe and I drank for hours. I drank alone for twenty minutes more before I realized he was gone. I made my way toward the front of the hall where I found Joe, arms flailing in high dudgeon, arguing with the cashier. If you've ever seen a baseball manager get into it with an umpire, then you've got an idea of what Joe—who today is a baseball coach at Northwestern—might have looked like.

Joe argued in English. The cashier argued in German. It was clear to me that neither understood a word the other was saying and that it was my job to step in as peacemaker. "Okay," I said, doing the best John Wayne impersonation my intoxication would allow, "what's the problem here?" That's when a bouncer appeared next to me and coldcocked me in the jaw.

The funny thing about getting knocked down by a sucker punch is that it doesn't hurt, not in the moment. There's a jolt, then you're on the floor. Then the pain starts to kick in. I barely had time to put those thoughts together before I was heave-hoed by the back of the pants as the bouncer sent me sprawling outside into the plaza. When I finally lifted my head, I found myself surrounded by hippies.

"Like, what'd they do to you, man?"

I didn't have time to answer—Joe came flying out the door a second later. We dusted ourselves off and staggered to our van. "What the hell just happened?" I asked.

"They'd only give me seventeen Deutschmarks for a

twenty-deutschmark traveler's check," he sputtered. "I'm sick and tired of getting killed on the goddamn exchange rate."

We drove north from Munich, bitter, angry, and depressed. It was already dark, so we stopped at the first patch of green grass we could find and pitched our tent for the night. In the morning, I stumbled out of the tent to pee and was happy to find a gatepost to steady myself while I finished my business. That's when I noticed the sign on the gate: *Dachau*. I sprinted back to the tent to wake Joe. "We just spent the night in a world-famous concentration camp."

Were we spooked? You bet. We gathered our stuff as quickly as possible, got into the van, and pressed the pedal to the floor. We didn't stop until we crossed the Rhine into France, where we comforted ourselves with the discovery of goose-liver pâté, chocolate éclairs, and Kronenbourg, a French beer to rival what we'd left behind in Germany.

REINHEITSGEBOT

In German, this means "purity order," which sounds pretty scary until you realize they're talking about beer. A Bavarian law enacted in 1516, the *Reinheitsgebot* declared that beer could only be brewed with water, barley, and hops. (If you're a home brewer, you might be wondering about the yeast. It wasn't an intentional omission: Amazingly, no one knew that yeast had anything to do with beer until the 1800s.)

The Bavarians considered the *Reinheitsgebot* to be so important that they refused to join Germany until the law was inscribed into the German constitution. In the years since, the law has expanded to allow other ingredients to creep into the brewing process, but among many modern beer makers, the *Reinheitsgebot* remains both a point of pride and a powerful marketing tool.

Beer Styles

When I was a kid, it seemed like there were only two kinds of beers in America: domestics and imports. The domestics were the yellow beers, like Budweiser, Pabst Blue Ribbon, and Miller High Life. Imports were exotic beers from foreign countries, like Heineken (the Netherlands) and Moosehead (Canada). Real men drank domestics. Beer snobs drank imports.

Like apples and oranges. Or so I thought. In hindsight, we were really choosing between apples and apple sauce. Today all of those beers are grouped together as *pale lagers*. Budweiser and Heineken are made the same way, more or less. They taste different because of the barley. European barley is starchy. Starchy is good for producing a lot of beer. American barley is heavier on proteins—not so good for making beer. In theory, you would need more barley to make an American beer than a European, and American beers would be the expensive ones. Joe Six-Pack might be drinking Kronenbourgs from France. God forbid. So American brewers take a few shortcuts, mixing barley with corn or rice to lower their costs, making your average American beer taste, you know, *different*. Not that there's anything wrong with different: Corn beer has been a part of South American culture since the Incas; and rice is the basis of Japan's tastiest brews. And if cutting a few corners helps make beer cheaper and more available to the common man, then so be it. For a long time, Americans rallied around this idea: As recently as the 1980s, people who drank imports were considered to be assholes.

We've come a long way since then. We haven't just moved past the debate on domestics versus imports; we're beyond pale lagers. The quickie mart at your local gas station probably carries ales or steam beers, or at the very least malt liquor. And while American brewers have always used sex to sell their beer, that used to mean breasts; now it means saying sexy things like "frost brewing" or "triple hops." Face it: We have all become assholes.

It's okay. Give yourself a hug. And be grateful that we live in a golden age of beer.

||||||||||||||||||||||||||||||||||||||||||||||||||||||||||||||||||||||||||||||||||||||||||||||||||||||||||||||||||||||||||||

A QUICK GUIDE TO BEER SNOBBERY

||||||||||||||||||||||||||||||||||||||||||||||||||||||||||||||||||||||||||||||||||||||||||||||||||||||||||||||||||||||||||||

There are dozens of ways to make beer in hundreds of flavors, and you'd have to be a fanatic to know them all. Fortunately, if you know a few basics, you can bullshit with the best of them. Here's a quick guide:

The first beers were basically *ales*: grains that were soaked in warm water until they fermented into beer. After a few centuries of experimentation, brewers figured out that they could adjust the flavor of the beer by roasting the grain first—the darker the roast, the darker the ale—and by adding honey or herbs. Sometime around the end of the first millennium A.D., they stumbled across *hops*, a weed that was previously considered useless, as it looked annoyingly similar to its cousin cannabis, only without the psychotropic benefits. But, added to beer, hops turned out to be the greatest thing since, well, beer, creating that distinctive taste we know and love.

A couple of hundred years later, some European monks discovered that storing the beer in a cold place for the winter gave it a crisper flavor. They called it *lager*, which is just German for "storage." It wasn't until 1840 that a couple of Germans, having rediscovered this old style of brewing, figured out that the cold storage caused the beer to be fermented by an entirely different kind of yeast that acted slowly from the bottom up instead of quickly from the top down. Two years later, in a daring act of corporate espionage, a Bavarian monk smuggled a vat of bottom-brewing beer into the Bohemian village of Pilsen (now the Czech city Plzeň). The Bohemians applied the lager technique to pale ale—creating *pale lager*—and so yellow beer was born. Today most of the world's beer is brewed using the "pilsner" technique, but in my opinion, no one has improved on the original Czech version, which you can still drink today as Pilsner Urquell. German lagers gradually morphed into *Märzen*, which is still consumed in dangerously large quantities every year at Oktoberfest.

The road has branched many times in different places. In England, British brewers had a lot of trouble making a great ale until they started mixing their not-so-great ales together to create a sum tastier than the parts, which they called *porter*. The Irish preferred a heartier porter they called *stout*, a formula mastered by Sir Arthur Guinness. In the American West, where refrigeration was an issue, settlers figured out how to fudge the lager process with steam, a process that's used today to make Anchor Steam. Creative brewers are still mining the past to rediscover all kinds of other styles invented out of convenience or necessity, from Dopplebocks (a thick lager brewed by monks as a Lenten meal replacement) to India Pale Ales (a high-alcohol brew designed to survive long voyages at sea).

THE ENERGY CENTER

"Work is the curse of the drinking classes."
—Oscar Wilde

 For two years after college, I repeated the same cycle: Europe, drinking good beer until the money ran out; then Chicago, where I worked for my dad, socking away enough money to get back to Europe again. If that sounds like a pretty good way to spend your life, you're right—it was—except for the nagging little voice in my head that kept reminding me that, sooner or later, I was going to have to grow up and get a real job.

During a philosophy class at Rockhurst we'd spent some time discussing Karl Marx's theory of alienation. I still don't have any idea what that theory was, but I remember the teacher—another Jesuit priest—talking about how so many people felt detached from their day jobs, living lives of quiet desperation. I promised myself in that classroom that I would be different, that I would find a career that suited the real me.

So one summer while in Switzerland, nearing the end of my bankroll, I sat down with a pen, a pad, and a beer and made a list of potential jobs. Then I crossed out the ones I thought I would hate, which was pretty much all of them. None of them seemed to jibe with who I was on a core level: a complete goof-off. Except for maybe one.

I'd gone a couple of times to see The Second City, Chicago's legendary improvisational theater. The word "legendary" gets thrown around too often, but in the case of Second City, it's deserved: For fifty years, the show has been a stepping-stone for several hundred of the funniest actors and comedians in show business.

THE SECOND CITY

Theater dates back thousands of years, so it's kind of strange to consider that improvisational sketch comedy is only about fifty years old. In the 1950s, a group of University of Chicago students got interested in reviving *commedia dell'arte*, an old Italian style of comedy that used bare-bones scripts and few props outside of a baton the actors used to whack one another called the "slapstick." The Compass Players, as they called themselves, opened a bar in Hyde Park, where they used theater games and short, improvised sketches to create a new, more immediate style of comedy. The theater only lasted about a year and a half, but in 1959 a few survivors formed a new group that would last a little longer. Invoking the kind of self-deprecating humor all too familiar to Chicagoans, they named themselves "The Second City," a term popularized by *The New Yorker* to describe our wee hamlet.

In the years since, Second City has expanded into Toronto (where *SCTV* was born), Detroit, Las Vegas, and Los Angeles and helped to launch the careers of hundreds of comic actors and co-mediennes. Here are a few alumni from the Chicago company whose names you might recognize: Alan Arkin, Jim Belushi, John Belushi, John Candy, Steve Carell, Dan Castellaneta, Stephen Colbert, Chris Farley, Tina Fey, Valerie Harper, Bonnie Hunt, Tim Kazurinsky, Robert Klein, Shelley Long, Tim Meadows, Bill Murray, Mike Myers, Bob Odenkirk, Harold Ramis, Joan Rivers, and Fred Willard.

I didn't have any desire to get into show business—that would have required actual ambition. What I saw in Second City was a bunch of guys and gals goofing around on stage. Even better, I was pretty sure they got paid for their troubles. I didn't know if I'd have any aptitude for improvisational comedy, aside from an innate goofiness, but at least I wouldn't be doing something I hated.

So when I got back to Chicago in the summer of 1973, I called The Second City. That is, I called the theater's box office. They referred me to something called the Players Workshop, where I found out that I'd gladly be accepted for as long as I was willing to pay them. Eighty-five dollars bought me thirteen Tuesday-night classes with Josephine Forsberg, a matriarch of the improv community and a disciple of Viola Spolin, who literally wrote the book on improv—she penned *Improvisation for the Theater*. (Not coincidentally, Viola was the mother of Paul Sills, one of the founders of Second City.)

I didn't hate it. For the first time in my life I actually worked hard at something. I was too clueless to be afraid. And it wasn't like I was surrounded by committed students of the craft; by day, my fellow students were ad men, city planners, and dental assistants. We were the class clowns, the chronic ne'er-do-wells, the slackers. Out of the twenty people in the workshop, maybe twelve of them were there by order of a therapist—many issues were worked out on the classroom stage. We met once a week, learning the basic fundamentals of improv, which more or less involves learning how to *not* try to be funny. Rule One is to be in the moment, reacting to your fellow players.

When that workshop ended I signed up for another. And another. And another. After a year of workshops, Josephine invited me to join something called the Children's Show, a relatively low-risk way to test my comedic chops in front of a Sunday-afternoon audience full of kids. Only she asked me to show up at 11:30 A.M., a few hours before the show was supposed to begin. When I arrived at the theater, she handed me a broom and a dustpan—I was expected to clean up after the regular Saturday-night show. "Welcome to the theater," Josephine said. (The sting was lessened a bit, years later, when I learned that David Mamet had begun his esteemed career as a Second City dishwasher.)

In 1974, after about a year with the Children's Show, I was invited to join the touring company. I might have made it earlier if not for a bar fight.

The old Comiskey Park, home to the White Sox until its demolition in the late 1980s, was a classic stadium, but you could drink there only during games—if you were looking for a beer before or after, you'd have to find another watering hole. The bar across the street, the venerable dive McCuddy's, was always packed to the gills, so the quest for beer sometimes meant an adventure on Chicago's South Side, which at that time was kind of a mob scene. As in, the *mob*.

MCCUDDY'S TUNNEL

McCuddy's was a bar that lived and died by the fortunes of Comiskey Park. Opened in 1910 by an owner who reportedly had inside knowledge of the plan to build a stadium across the street, it was demolished in 1988 to make room for the new Comiskey. Rumor was that a secret tunnel once connected the bar to the visiting team's locker room, luring opposing players into bad behavior: Babe Ruth was supposed to have snuck into McCuddy's for hot dogs and beers between games of a doubleheader. Another rumor during the 1970s suggested the tunnel served as a conduit for ferrying in-game beers to the legendary announcer Harry Caray, a free spirit during his time with the Sox who allegedly liked to keep his classic pipes well lubricated.

|||||||||||||||||||||||||||||||||||||||||||||||||||||||||||||||||||||||||||||||||||||||||||||||||||||||||||||||||||||||||||||||

The night before my first audition for Second City's touring company, I went to a White Sox game with three friends. I could have just gone home after the game and rested up for the next day, but I knew I'd rest a lot better after a few more beers. McCuddy's was too crowded, so we found a bar a couple of blocks away that didn't look too dangerous.

We quietly took our seats at the bar, carefully avoiding eye contact with any of the other customers—in this neighborhood, everyone was a potential mobster. Despite our efforts to be inconspicuous, we still got a memorable welcome from one regular, a ringer for Robert De Niro in *Mean Streets*, who introduced us to his version of the kids' game "Duck, Duck, Goose." It wasn't "duck, duck, goose" but "fuck you, fuck you, fuck you, fuck YOU!" The almost–De Niro punctuated his final YOU by punching my friend Mac in the face, knocking him off his barstool.

One of my friends, Joe Farmar, was far braver than me. He leapt to Mac's defense—at least he started to, until he remembered where we were. By then it was too late. Bottles were broken. Chairs went flying across the room. Pool cues were cracked in half and swung wildly. We were in the middle of a full-on bar fight.

GEORGE'S TIPS ON SURVIVING A BAR FIGHT

1. Avoid the fight. For me, that means making an exaggerated show of rolling up my sleeves and announcing "Here comes the gun show." Although I might avoid the firearm reference if my potential adversary looks like he could possibly have a gun and is at all twitchy.

2. Have more friends than they do. You ever hear the one about the British explorer in Africa who fought off a hungry lion with just a club? He would have been in trouble had his club not numbered in the dozens. Unless you're Patrick Swayze in *Road House*, you always want to bring superior numbers to a bar fight.

3. Trust the authorities. Bouncers are there for a reason—to keep the bar from getting wrecked. As a result, most bar fights don't last very long.

4. Fall on the ground and cry. And if that doesn't work, act like you're mentally disabled. A moment of political incorrectness can sometimes save you weeks in the hospital.

Finally, under no circumstances should you ever say, "Please, not in the face—I've got an audition tomorrow." Trust me on this one.

One of the positive things about bar fights is that they're generally over quickly. Bar management may not care a lick about your well-being—they're happily destroying your liver, aren't they?—but the cost of replacing broken chairs and pool sticks can add up in a hurry. Fortunately, our fight stuck to form: The bartender knew the instigators and shoved them out the front door. Several hours later, he managed to get rid of us, assuring us for the thousandth time that no one was out there waiting for us.

The thugs were long gone, but I still had to audition for the touring company looking like something out of a horror movie. I walked with a limp. One of my eyes was swollen shut. I'd like to tell you how I overcame adversity and aced the audition. The truth is I was back to doing the Children's Show, wearing pancake makeup so as not to terrify the kids.

My disappointment only lasted a month, as the entire touring company *defected*. During a gig at an Ohio seafood joint called Pickle Bills, the restaurant's management convinced the Second City players to quit the touring show and perform at the restaurant full-time. Emergency auditions were held to replace them, and this time I landed a spot.

I'd expected my father to be surprised when I told him I was quitting the office—somehow I'd kept the workshops and the shows a secret from him. Or so I thought. It turned out he already knew. A friend of his saw my picture in a group photo posted outside Second City's theater on Wells Street. Dad and my sister Kathy even snuck into the theater one Sunday afternoon to see me perform in the Children's Show. My father, a rare bird in that he was a Midwestern heterosexual who loved opera and the navy, was already predisposed to love camaraderie and a good show. He sent me off with his blessings.

After nearly a year with the touring company, I was at last asked to join the resident company on the main stage. Finally getting up close to the performers I'd admired for so long, I learned two things: (1) they were unquestionably comedic geniuses; and (2) most of them were total lushes.

We didn't have to show up to work until four o'clock, making it the perfect job for drinkers. We'd spend a few hours performing shows with names like "Freud Slipped Here" and "I Remember Dada." When the curtain came down, usually around eleven o'clock, we'd start drinking. The best perk that came with being in the resident company was free beer: We were given full access to a perpetually tapped keg of Stroh's at the theater's bar. Greedy drunks that we were, we'd also fill ten-ounce tumbler glasses with cognac, schnapps, or whatever else we could find behind the bar. Both policies were abused so badly that the keg was eventually untapped and locks were installed on the liquor cabinets. Similar locks were later installed on the refrigerator to keep us away from the whipped cream, but not before fellow performers Danny Breen and Jim Belushi incorporated the canisters into an act. The sketch, if you can call it that—Danny and Jim took improv suggestions from the crowd while happily gassing themselves with nitrous—was performed only once, and it ended with the performers on the floor, giggling incoherently, getting booed by the few audience members who hadn't run for the exits.

Just your typical workday.

WHAT IS IMPROV?

The Second City performers were almost all heavy drinkers—after the show. Improv took too much mental agility to risk getting wasted beforehand.

One night during a performance, a rat wandered across the stage—renovations to the theater had apparently disturbed a nest full of them. Most of the humans in the building shrieked and looked ready to flee the building. Until Tim Kazurinsky and I grabbed army helmets and prop rifles and launched into an Elmer

Fudd "Kill da wabbit" routine, incorporating our new furry friend into the act.

But the best in the business might have been the legendary Del Close, who served Second City as a performer, director, and teacher when he wasn't touring with the Merry Pranksters or hanging out with the Grateful Dead.

Del was once invited to a formal party and, having no tux, raided the Second City's musty prop room until he found one that looked passable. He passed well enough to be introduced to the playwright Tennessee Williams, with whom he shook hands. A cockroach, who until then had been living happily inside the prop tuxedo, crawled out of his sleeve and onto the hand that had penned *A Streetcar Named Desire* and *Cat on a Hot Tin Roof.*

"I beg your pardon," Del said without missing a beat, plucking the roach from Williams's arm. "I believe *that* belongs to me."

After starting our drinking at the theater, we'd sometimes go to bars: the Old Town Ale House, or the Blues Bar, a place John Belushi and Dan Aykroyd set up in an old carriage house while filming *The Blues Brothers* so that they'd have a cool place to unwind. But most of the time, we drank at home.

Home was a cheap but massive apartment we nicknamed the "Energy Center." It was a pretty greystone with hardwood floors that I shared with two other guys, allowing us to reside stylishly in an elegant part of town.

And we destroyed it.

The name "Energy Center" was ironic—something about

the place seemed to inspire laziness. The landlord was a hypothetical. No one ever showed the wherewithal to call him, no matter what went wrong with the place. (When a Wisconsin-shaped piece of plaster fell from the ceiling, we used magic markers to label the major cities and points of attraction.)

It was a long, narrow apartment, and garbage tended to flow toward the kitchen in the back. Piles of sixteen-ounce empties became load-bearing walls (the load being more beer cans), a labyrinth that Danny Breen, who had the room nearest the kitchen, had to navigate to find his bed. Branching corridors led to the sink and refrigerator. Cooking was clearly not a possibility, although Bernadette, my future wife and back then fellow Second City member, actually gave it a few tries. What she wouldn't do is set foot in the bathroom, given the level of filth, but we worked around it: Once, when she needed to bathe before a show, I carried her into the bathroom, set her in the tub, and retrieved her when she'd finished.

Our landlord sent an agent, a fussy man, when we were late with the rent, which occasionally forced us to tidy up. But the only times the apartment would approach actual cleanliness were before our two annual parties: a Christmas bash and a summertime gathering that coincided with Chicago's big art fair. Our cleaning frenzies were times of discovery: We'd open the refrigerator in December and find a watermelon that had been there since July. (At least we hoped it was a watermelon.) Once we found a couch. An actual couch, buried under a pile of newspapers. We stared in amazement for hours—given how much we all loved couches, we might as well have found the lost treasure of the Aztecs. But whatever gains we'd made in the hygiene department were generally erased—and then some—by the time the evening's festivities came to an end.

The Energy Center served as sort of a dorm for Second City troupers and stagehands who rotated into the bedrooms. Sometimes the bedrooms were used by nonresidents. Jim Belushi, who was living at home with his parents, once brought a lady friend back to the apartment. He also brought a stack of 33s, which he placed on the stereo. You had to admire Jim's nerve and optimism: Not only did he want to get carnal in one of our bedrooms, but he actually asked us to flip the records over to their B-sides when the music stopped. Which we gladly did, just not with the albums he brought with him. According to Jim, he was nearing orgasm when the soundtrack to *The Wizard of Oz* kicked in. Hearing the Wicked Witch scream "I'll get you, my pretty!" turned out to be the audio equivalent of saltpeter.

We finally fell so behind in the rent that the fussy guy showed up to evict us. He entered with a sympathetic expression that quickly turned to sputtering rage when he saw the apartment's condition. "You . . ." he managed. "You . . . You're definitely out. OUT!"

"Yeah," Danny said sadly. "We know. Sorry."

Serving Beer at Home

Beer cozies. Beer caddies. Beer carriers, thermal bags, and mini–thermal bags. Beer hats, as in hats that hold beer. Pocket holsters with quick-can release. I own all of these things. Once you get saddled with a reputation as the Beer Guy, you've given your family, friends, and professional acquaintances all of the ideas they'll ever need to buy you a gift. For the rest of your life.

Which isn't a bad thing, except for the times you get a gift that an obvious nonbeer drinker thought you would find interesting. Boysenberry beer. *Buttermilk* beer. "That's so *interesting*," is usually the best I can manage. "So you're saying that no hops at all were killed in the production of this beer?" Or "bier paper"—writing paper made out of beer. I remember eyeing that gift for a good ten minutes before giving up. "You got me—how am I going to drink it?"

COLD BEER IN A MINUTE OR LESS

Unless you're British, you probably aren't a big fan of warm beer. Most American beers taste best cold—around 42° F is ideal. European lagers can stand to be a little warmer, maybe 48° F or so. But what do you do when you're out of cold beer?

The easy answer is not to run out of cold beer: You can always maintain a backup supply in a dedicated beer fridge. But if you don't have a beer fridge, you're not quite shit out of luck: Better living—or at least a colder beer—can be yours through the application of modern chemistry.

The obvious choice is to put warm beer in the freezer. It's not a terrible idea—you'll get a beer that's passably cold after about twenty or twenty-five minutes. Just don't forget that you've put the beers in the freezer: Frozen beers have a bad habit of exploding, creating huge messes and, worse, wasting perfectly good beer.

If twenty minutes waiting for a beer feels like twenty hours of real time, you can cut the time in half by putting the beer on ice. But chilling a beer on ice is a little like sleeping on stones—it's hard for the beer to get comfortable. There are too many nooks and crannies forming pockets of above-freezing air for the beer to cool at peak performance.

You can solve the nooks and crannies issue by pouring water

on top of the ice. Now your beer is completely immersed in a frozen bath. Employ this trick and you'll have cold beer in five to six minutes.

But the benefits of science don't have to end there. The coldest water can get (without freezing) is 32° Fahrenheit. You can help the process along by mixing salt into the water, lowering its freezing temperature. With enough salt—we're talking a couple of cups—you can actually get the temperature of the bath below zero: You're just a couple of minutes away from a cold beer!

But what are you going to do, stand around for two minutes? You might as well spin the beer while you're waiting. Thanks to one of the many laws of physics, the spinning motion causes the can to lose its heat even faster. With an ice-salt bath and a little bit of elbow grease, you can be drinking a cold beer in under two minutes.

If you're strapped for salt or ice (or are too drunk and/or lazy to deal with finding them) but have access to basic fire safety equipment, you can always use a fire extinguisher. It's been reported that a full blast of CO_2 can ice down an entire six-pack in about three minutes.

The best beer-related gift came from my wife: For our fifteenth anniversary, she had a keg tap installed on our patio. Does the woman know romance or what? Draft beer straight from the keg, twenty-four/seven, at least until our kids got wise. "Can I have some beer, Daddy?" my daughter started asking me around her fifteenth birthday.

"Not until you're done with your homework, honey." Parenting sometimes requires a firm hand.

BABY BEER?

In America it's considered irresponsible (or worse) to give beer to kids. In Belgium, it's just good common sense. Table beer—a brew with less than half the alcohol content of a regular beer—has long been served to kids as young as eight or nine. Some schools even serve the stuff in their cafeterias, heartened by a study showing that 99 percent of Belgian children prefer table beer to the chemically carbonated, high-fructose corn-syrup–flavored sodas that we feed the kids in America. Crazy? Maybe. But can a mild beer be any worse than a Coke? Or, for that matter, Ritalin?

I'm not a totally irresponsible parent. When my son decided to throw his high-school graduation party in our backyard, my wife and I agonized over whether or not to buy the kids a keg. We weren't morally opposed to the idea—as high-school graduates ourselves, we were pretty sure there was going to be some drinking—but that didn't mean we wanted to be the ones serving beer to minors, especially minors with car keys.

But we eventually caved in, after securing a few promises from our son in regards to responsibility, and installed a keg of light beer underneath the home tap. Then Bernadette and I hid in our bedroom, praying that we hadn't made a terrible mistake.

When we woke up the next morning, Bernadette and I smiled at each other. There hadn't been any calls in the middle of the night. Our kids were all safe in bed. Whew! We got away with it.

I walked outside, wondering if there'd be enough left in the keg for me to have a breakfast beer. The patio and lawn were covered with dozens of empty bottles of vodka, scotch, and tequila. Like the kids needed our help.

THE HOME KEG

The idea of a keg at home used to seem mildly ridiculous. Actually, it probably still does, unless your home is a fraternity house. But it shouldn't be: A home keg is an easy way to turn pretty much any occasion—from watching a game to enhancing your breakfast cereal—into a special occasion.

It wasn't that long ago when the only kegs you could find were filled with Budweiser or Heineken, maybe Pilsner Urquell if you lived near a specialty liquor store. Not anymore. Most liquor stores stock a wide range of kegs. If you happen to live near a BevMo, you can find just about anything from Abita to Widmer.

If you don't have the money to shell out for a full-fledged kegerator, you can build your own with a small refrigerator and a conversion kit. If you don't have the space, you can buy miniature "pony" kegerators. And if you don't have the money or the space for a kegerator, real or makeshift, there are plenty of minikeg dispensers that will fit on a countertop and run you less than the cost of a juicer.

||||||||||||||||||||||||||||||||||||||||||||||||||||||||||||||||||||||||||||||||||||||||||||||||||||||||||||||||||||||||||||||||||||||||||||||||||||||||||||||||||||||||||||||||||

BEER
AND THE LAW

"I often sit back and think, 'I wish I'd done that,'
and find out later that I already have."
—Richard Harris

 I read an article recently about pairing beer with different foods. To paraphrase those Virginia Slims ads from the 1970s, we've come a long way, baby. In the '70s, the most I knew was that beer paired well with chips and nuts. Or shots. And, occasionally, regrettable behavior.

Case in point: Not too long after I'd graduated college some friends and I got together for an evening of poker playing. There might have been more drinking than card playing, which explains why I left the game broke. My consolation prize was a six-pack for the road.

Yes, we all knew driving while intoxicated was, you know, *wrong*, but it didn't have the same stigma back then—

Possibly the only safe way to drink and drive.

breathalyzers and Mothers Against Drunk Driving were still ten years away. So I cracked open a beer on the way to the car, and another when I hit Chicago's Loop. "Hit" is actually the perfect word, as I managed to drive through a row of lampposts.

DRUNK DRIVING

Back in the 1970s, your blood alcohol content needed to be 0.15 (that's 15 percent!) or higher for you to be considered too drunk to drive. That number has (justifiably) been halved since then: In most of the United States, 0.08 is the legal limit.

Whatever America's politics, we're all liberals when it comes to beer—our 8 percent is among the highest legal thresholds in the world. Beer meccas Germany and Austria will arrest you for blood alcohol content over 0.05.

Ironically, the Czech Republic—one of the richest beer cultures in the world—has a zero-tolerance law: A single drink is enough to get you arrested for drunk driving. Then again, considering that the Czechs drink more beer per person than anyone else in the world maybe that isn't so ironic.

||||||||||||||||||||||||||||||||||||||||||||||||||||||||||||||||||||||||||||||||||||||||||||||||||||||||||||||||||||||||||||||||||||||||

When the police found me by the side of the road, I was busily changing a tire. "What are you doing there, son?" one of them asked.

"Well, Officer, I'm changing my tire."

"Riiiiiight. Did you happen to notice that *all four* of your tires are blown?"

"Huh. You guys wouldn't happen to have three extra spares?"

The police put me in the squad car and took me to jail, where they told me I could make a phone call. I was too terrified to call my father, so I called my friend Joe Keenan.

By the time one of the guards told me Joe had arrived, I'd been sleeping in the cell for a while. Joe laughed when he saw me—the prison cot had imprinted a waffle pattern on the side of my face. I would have laughed too, if I hadn't noticed that Joe had brought his father with him. All of a sudden, I turned into Eddie Haskell from *Leave It to Beaver*. "Oh, hello, Mr. Keenan."

"Hello, George," his father said sternly. "Why don't you tell me what happened?"

When I was finished telling my story, Mr. Keenan nodded slowly. "Well," he said, "I guess us Campion guys have to stick together." Joe's dad and I had attended the same high school. I was still drunk, and I felt like an idiot, but I had to smile. For the first time in my life, I felt like I'd crossed that mystical bridge between child and adult. Mr. Keenan wasn't treating me like a dumb kid with beer oozing from his pores and a waffle imprint on his face; he was treating me like a peer.

IRISH HANDCUFFS

Years ago, at the White Horse Tavern in Manhattan's Greenwich Village, a woman approached me and asked me for an autograph. I would have been happy to oblige, except that I had a beer in each hand. "Ah," she said. "Irish handcuffs."

Years later, I accompanied my Irish mother to a function at her local country club. As I guided her across the room with one hand, steadied by a beer in my other, it dawned on me: Now *these* are Irish handcuffs.

A couple of weeks later, my case went to court. I felt anxious waiting for my name to be called. The anxiety grew with each hour—when the hell would it be my turn? The judge finished with every case except mine, then excused himself and left the room. A new judge replaced him.

"Well, Mr. Wendt," said the new judge, "I see you've just turned twenty-one."

"Yes, Your Honor."

"Your first hours of legal drinking and you've already broken the law. What do you do for a living?"

"I'm a student, Your Honor. At Rockhurst College in Kansas City."

"Oh really? Do you happen to know Father Frank Carey?"

"Yes, Your Honor. Father Carey is the director of admissions there. Before that he was director of admissions at my high school."

"You went to Campion Jesuit?"

"Class of '66, Your Honor."

"I see," the judge said. "You might be interested to know that I graduated Campion in 1951."

"I went to Mount Carmel!" the bailiff chimed in.

"I went to Leo!" added one of the clerks.

I suddenly understood why my case was the last of the day. I was part of Chicago's Catholic school mafia, and the fix was in.

"Case dismissed!" the judge declared. The policemen who'd testified against me left the courtroom shaking their heads.

Sadly, Campion Jesuit is no more. I once tried to revisit the place, only to discover that it was surrounded by a concertina-wire fence. I wasn't going to let anything like a

fence keep me from having my *A Separate Peace* moment at
the old prep school, so I moved closer. A loudspeaker blared
to life: "STEP AWAY FROM THE PERIMETER!"

In a moment of sheer poetry, I discovered that Campion
Jesuit is now a prison.

THE GREATEST BEER HEIST IN HISTORY

In 2007, a daring thief drove into Dublin's Guinness brewery in
broad daylight, hitched his truck to a trailer loaded for delivery,
and slipped out the gate into rush-hour traffic. The score: one
hundred and eighty barrels each of Guinness and Budweiser,
and another ninety kegs of Carlsberg. Estimated street value:
$235,000. The police would eventually arrest a man and charge
him with possession of one of the stolen kegs, but most of the
beer was never recovered.

(More Than) One Hundred Ways to Say That You're Drunk

I always hear people talk about the Eskimos having nine or ten words for snow. Count me among the unimpressed: I can think of over a hundred English words and expressions for being drunk without breaking a sweat.

1. Annihilated
2. Bashed
3. Befuddled
4. Bent

5. Bibulous

6. Blasted

7. Blithering

8. Blitzed

9. Blotto

10. Bolloxed

11. Bombed

12. Boozed up

13. Butt-wasted

14. Buzzed

15. Clobbered

16. Cockeyed

17. Comatose

18. Crapulous

19. Crocked

20. Decimated

21. Drucking funk

22. Drunk as a . . . (skunk, fiddler, lord, etc.)

23. Far gone

24. Feeling no pain

25. Fired up

26. Floored

27. Fried

28. FUBAR!

29. Fucked up

30. Gassed

31. Ginned up

32. Gonzo

33. Good to go

34. Groggy

35. Half gone

36. Hammered

37. Hooched up

38. Hung one on

39. Impaired

40. In one's cups

41. In rare form

42. Inebriated

43. Intoxicated

44. Invincible

45. Jacked

46. Juiced

47. Keyed

48. Knocked silly

49. Lathered

50. Leathered

51. Legless

52. Liquored up

53. Lit

54. Loaded

55. Looped

56. Lubricated

57. Marinated

58. Massacred

59. Messed up

60. Mottled

61. Nuked

62. Obliterated

63. Off the wagon

64. On a bender

65. On fire

66. Out of it

67. Pickled

68. Pie-eyed

69. Piffled

70. Pissed

71. Plastered

72. Plotzed

73. Potted

74. Put one on

75. Reeked

76. Reeling

77. Ripped

78. Rocked

79. Ruined

80. Rummy

81. Sauced

82. Shellacked

83. Shit-faced

84. Slammed

85. Slaughtered

86. Sloppy

87. Sloshed

88. Soaked

89. Sozzled

90. Smashed

91. Steaming

92. Stewed

93. Stinko

94. Stoned

95. Stoopid

96. Tanked

97. Temulent

98. Three sheets to the wind

99. Tied one on

100. Tight

101. Tipsy

102. Toasted

103. Trashed

104. Trousered

105. Under the influence

106. Under the table

107. Unsober

108. Wasted

109. Worse for wear

110. Wrecked

111. Zombied

112. Zozzled

BEER AND ROMANCE: THE ORIGINAL "BROMANCE"

"Give me a woman who loves beer and I will
conquer the world."
—Kaiser Wilhelm

I loved Second City and everything it stood for, but the feeling wasn't always mutual. While I got plenty of laughs onstage, when it came to creating my own material—something all of the performers were required to do—the show's producers were worried that I lacked a clear comic voice. I called it "sucking out loud." After a year with the resident company, they sent me back to the minors—the touring company—to work on my game.

At the time, the touring company had a long-term arrangement with Chateau Louise, a resort fifty miles west of Chicago. It was less a resort than twenty or so trailers cobbled together to look like a resort. Pretty depressing. Along with fellow performers like Tim Kazurinsky and Bernadette Birkett, I commuted back and forth each day, usually in my car.

And I hated my car.

This wasn't always the case. Originally I loved my green '73 VW Super Beetle. When I wrecked it in an accident—I was one of the middle cars in a six-car pileup—I couldn't wait to get it back. My father, who had a relationship with a body shop, offered to take care of the repairs for me. But the repairs seemed to take forever—every week I'd call the shop, and every week I got the same answer: "Maybe next week."

Finally, they told me the car was ready for pickup. I knew something was weird as soon as I walked into the garage. None of the mechanics were working; instead, they were staring at me strangely and looked like they were trying to keep from cracking up. Then I saw the car. On my father's orders, they'd replaced the front and back of the tiny Beetle with a Rolls-Royce grille and bumpers. I struggled to speak. "My car didn't . . ."

"It does now!" laughed one of the mechanics.

I thought it was about the worst thing that ever happened to me. I was ridiculed every time I stopped at a traffic light. But my father honestly believed that I would love it, and I didn't have the heart to disappoint him. So every day

Amazing, I know.

I drove my laughingstock of a car the hundred miles round-trip to Chateau Louise, ignoring the taunts and jibes from fellow motorists.

The theater at Chateau Louise was a five-hundred-seat monstrosity that was rarely if ever full, especially during Wednesday matinees, when the management imported old ladies from nearby nursing homes to fill the seats. When the elderly were unavailable, they turned to mental institutions. The most unsettling show I ever performed was for a group of psychiatric patients, many of whom had stitches in their heads from recent lobotomies. It wasn't the scars that scared me as much as their reaction: They laughed wildly at all the straight lines and remained utterly stone-faced during the jokes.

We once did the Wednesday matinee for an audience of two. "We can't do this," I insisted, looking over the nearly empty room. "Way too humiliating." My fellow players agreed. So we all kicked in a few bucks and came up with about sixty dollars to buy the couple a fancy lunch. Then we drew straws to see who would convince them to take the money and come back for the evening show. Castmate Nancy McCabe-Kelly picked the short straw.

Nancy did her best to explain the situation to the couple, a husband and wife in their late forties. They just stared at her blankly. "But we drove here all the way from Wisconsin," the husband explained. "We told the sitter we'd be home by six. It's our twenty-fifth anniversary, you know."

Nancy returned backstage with the money. "We're doing the show." It actually wound up being one of the most entertaining shows I've ever been a part of—whoever wasn't performing onstage in the sketch joined the audience, making cracks about the performers. Afterward, we took the couple out for beers. Talk about an intimate night at the theater.

But while my demotion to the touring show was professionally disappointing, at least it was steady work with a great group of players. And without it I never would have met a very funny (and very hot) blonde named Bernadette Birkett.

Actually, that probably isn't true. The more amazing thing is that I didn't meet Bernadette earlier. We grew up just a few miles away from each other, the children of Catholic families in neighboring parishes, which put us both on a circuit that ran through Phil Smidt's restaurant—home to lake perch and crossed frogs' legs—on many Friday nights during Lent. When life wasn't all about self-denial, Bernadette's dad used to take her family to the Rainbow Cone Ice Cream Shop, just three blocks from my house. And Bernadette, like my sister Kathy, was a hostess in the Illinois pavilion at the 1965 World's Fair.

||||||||||||||||||||||||||||||||||||||||||||||||||||||||||||||||||||||||||||||||||||||||||||||||||||||||||||||||||||||||||||||||||||||||||||||||||||

In ancient Egypt, offering a sip of beer to a lady was considered a marriage proposal.

||||||||||||||||||||||||||||||||||||||||||||||||||||||||||||||||||||||||||||||||||||||||||||||||||||||||||||||||||||||||||||||||||||||||||||||||||||

But Bernadette and I didn't meet until we were both members of Second City's touring company. I was smitten by her blue eyes; she was intrigued by my resistance to wearing underwear. (I liked to go "commando style" in those days—comfortable for me, but not so much for my fellow footlighters, especially during our rapid-fire wardrobe changes.) She was also a lot more mature than me—while we were (and still are) about the same age, by the time we met she already had one ex-husband and two children.

We began to fall in love during an engagement at our hometown's Ravinia Festival, where our show would follow the Chicago Symphony—or, as we like to say, the Chicago Symphony opened for *us*. On July 4, 1976—America's Bicentennial—we finally went on our first date, to the 2350 Pub on Lincoln Avenue. According to Bernadette, she knew we were in love because neither of us could form a simple sentence. Then again, it could have been the beer.

A reason to be grateful for the Chateau Louise.

BEER GOGGLES

Beer is the third most popular beverage on earth—behind water and tea—but when it comes to romance, beer is number one. Water's not going to help you overcome shyness. And tea's never going to increase your attractiveness.

Studies have shown that drinking does, in fact, make potential partners look 25 percent better than they would if you were sober. Beer: making the world a more beautiful place.

Two years and four days later, on 7/8/78, Bernadette and I were married. The wedding was wonderful—or what we can remember of it. My friend Joe Farmar, to no one's great surprise, ditched the ceremony and convinced the staff at the Como Inn, site of our reception, to open the bar while Bernadette and I were still exchanging vows. The end result was a bar bill that was three times larger than what we spent on food and rentals combined. Unfortunately (or maybe fortunately), our wedding photographer's car was robbed during the party—nearly all of his film was stolen, eliminating most of the visual evidence that the wedding ever took place.

MY FAVORITE WEDDING TOAST

I stole this from my friend and fellow Second City veteran Matt Dwyer: "Sixty-three percent of marriages end in divorce. The other thirty-seven percent end in death," I say, raising my glass. "I hope you die!"

Bernadette and I decided to honeymoon for two weeks in Amsterdam. We both loved the city—the canals, the art, the beer—but after two or three days, we were feeling restless. Like the crazy kids we were, we rented a car and drove toward France. We spent a few romantic days touring the Ardennes, leaving no World War II battle site unexplored. ("Look how many people died *here*, honey!")

THE ORIGIN OF THE HONEYMOON

In ancient Babylon—the place most historians consider to be the birthplace of beer—it was customary for the father of the bride to gift a newly married couple with a month's supply of mead—honey ale—to help jump-start the business of producing heirs. Given that the Babylonians used a lunar calendar, it didn't take long for this month of drunken marital bed-breaking to earn the name "honeymoon."

Another phrase that may have evolved from beer? *Rule of thumb*. Some etymologists claim that the term comes from the practice among brewers of sticking one's thumb into a vat of fermenting beer to check the temperature—too cold and the grain wouldn't germinate, too hot and the yeast would die. This explanation has been contradicted by other etymologists, who claim "rule of thumb" refers to the maximum size of the rod an Englishman could use to beat his wife. When it comes to romance, it's hard to top the English!

We eventually wound up in a small village in the Champagne region. It was Bastille Day—the French Fourth of July—so we decided to treat ourselves to a fine French meal at a local *auberge*. We thought that meant we should order some of the exotic French cuisine we'd heard about, like escargot and animal organs. Big mistake, I realized too late, watching a plate of *steak frites* float by. But we forged ahead with the snails and sweetbreads, learning along the way that "squab" meant "pigeon." The experience was further enhanced by the *auberge's* charming owner, who spent most of our meal hitting on my brand new bride as if I weren't there.

At least the beer was good—Kronenbourg—so of course I drank six of them. Plus an after-dinner Armagnac, topped off with an espresso. The rest of the day felt kind of like a dream . . .

EXT. FRENCH MOUNTAIN ROAD—BASTILLE DAY

George pilots a tiny Fiat—a stick-shift—up a narrow mountain road. He appears to be turning green. His new wife, Bernadette, smiles happily out the window.

BERNADETTE

That *auberge* owner sure was nice, wasn't he, George?

GEORGE

Honey . . . I don't feel so well.

BERNADETTE

Poor baby. The escargot?

GEORGE

No . . .

BERNADETTE

Are you coming down with a cold?

GEORGE

No, I feel really bad. I think we should go back.

BERNADETTE

To the *auberge*?

GEORGE

To Chicago.

BERNADETTE

I told you two weeks was a long time to spend on a honeymoon.

GEORGE

I think I'm having a heart attack!

BERNADETTE

What was that, honey?

GEORGE

I can't breathe.

George pulls the car into a gas station. He exits the vehicle and lies down on the pavement. He struggles to breathe.

BERNADETTE

Do you want me to call a doctor?

GEORGE

Too . . . late . . . Get me a . . . priest.

When the ambulance arrived, I was lying down in the middle of a gas station driveway. Bernadette rode with me to the hospital.

If you're a believer in socialized medicine and you want to give yourself a gut-check, try the emergency room of a French hospital on Bastille Day. It was absolute chaos. None of the medical staff spoke English, so someone had to track down the English teacher from the local high school to translate. Clearly perturbed by the interruption to his holiday, the teacher nodded impatiently as the doctor said a few things in French. "The doctors, they want to perform some more tests on you," he translated. "And more important, someone has to move your car."

A driver took Bernadette back to the gas station, where a line of cars honked angrily. It's hard to blame them—no one could reach the pumps thanks to a green Fiat, which I'd parked in the middle of the driveway. I have to give my wife a lot of credit: She didn't let the horns—or the stress of her brand-new husband's hospitalization and possibly imminent death—get in the way of learning how to drive a stickshift, which she'd never done before. She taught herself on the fly, despite the fact that the instruction book in the glove compartment was written in Italian.

Once the car had been moved to the side of the road, Bernadette phoned the hospital. "They want to keep me here overnight," I told her.

"Well, where am I supposed to stay?" she asked.

"I don't know, but definitely not that *auberge*. I don't trust that place."

One of the doctors volunteered to let Bernadette spend the night at his *grand chateau*. At least the *auberge* owner wouldn't be hitting on her all night, I thought. Turns out I should have been more worried about the doctor.

Grand chateau turns out to be French for "forty-room castle with servants and horses." Not just horses roaming about, either—the chateau had its own indoor equestrian facility. And then there was Dr. Michél Curie, who was handsome, soulful, a descendant of his nation's most famous scientist, and extremely rich. Whatever language difficulties we'd experienced at the hospital turned out to have been temporary—Dr. Curie spent much of the night charming Bernadette with perfectly understandable English. "I love America," he said. "Especially Texas. Cowboys! Bang, bang!" He told her how his mother, ten years earlier, got lost in New York City without any money and unable to speak a word of English. A sympathetic taxi driver took her home and fed her and then helped her reunite with her fellow travelers. And now, thanks to Bernadette's current distress, the Good Doctor finally had a chance to repay the kindness.

The servants were off for the holiday, so Dr. Curie took it upon himself to make her dinner: steak frites, of course, with French fries Bernadette described as the best she'd ever tasted. They washed the meal down with a half-bottle of fine scotch.

· · ·

The next morning, I awoke at the hospital looking like someone who'd been poked, prodded, and blood-sampled all night long. Bernadette was refreshed and beaming, having just experienced some high-class French hospitality.

"Your wife is a very charming woman," said Dr. Curie.

"So I've discovered," I replied. "Have you figured out what's wrong with me?"

"Ah yes, your condition." He studied the chart. "It appears you have suffered an anxiety attack."

Now, I'm no doctor, but I think if I'd skipped the espresso and stuck to the Kronenbourg our honeymoon might've ended a bit differently. Live and learn. In any case, after receiving my diagnosis we recovered the Fiat, drove straight to Frankfurt, and caught the next plane home.

Beer Is (Not) Just for Boys

There are more than 6.5 billion people in the world, and more than half of them are women. Of those billions of women, approximately thirty-four of them love to drink beer.

Okay, I'm exaggerating, but you probably know what I mean. As my wife, Bernadette, likes to point out, drinking beer is like walking into a men's locker room. She's not referring to the taste (or at least I don't think she is), but to beer's reputation and culture, which is decidedly masculine.

One problem is advertising: Not only are beer commercials targeted at men, but they occasionally veer into territory that women find offensive. Another problem: men, who when they drink occasionally veer into behavior that everyone finds embarrassing. These are not selling points for our friend beer. Unfortunately, these problems are completely unsolvable, since neither sexist advertising nor embarrassing behavior is going anywhere anytime soon.

"So George," you're probably wondering, "what can I do to help the world, specifically to help the non–beer lover in my life overcome her resistance to beer?" The answer, as an environmentalist might tell you, is to think globally but act locally. Here are a few tips to help you help your special someone learn to love beer.

1. Become a Beer Chef

Most women love men who can cook. So why not become a man who can cook . . . with beer?

Beer's unique combination of yeast, hops, and alcohol makes it a phenomenal cooking tool. It's a great marinade for meats and seafood and a tasty ingredient in glazes and barbecue sauces. You can use it to fine-tune batters for fried foods, to add punch to potato salad, to simmer sausages, or steam shellfish. Use it instead of water to make homemade pizza dough, or tell her you're going to make her Belgium's most famous gourmet dish (next to the waffles): *carbonnade à la flamande*, a supersexy name for beef stewed in Belgian ale.

Hell, a beer can be a meal in and of itself. Hungry? Have a pint of Guinness. Still hungry? Have another. You're not going to need a third.

2. Beer Is Beautiful

There are women who will turn down beef stew. But I've never met a woman who will turn down a pedicure. Offer to pamper her feet salon-style. Then fill a bucket with beer and tell her to start soaking her hoofers. It's no joke—there's a salon in Chicago that actually offers this on the menu. The alcohol is a natural antiseptic, and the yeast softens calloused skin.

If feet aren't your thing, there's always her hair. It's been a secret among stylists for centuries that beer—loaded with B-vitamins—is an excellent conditioner that will add body, shine, and silkiness to your mane. Just make sure you rinse her hair in beer *before* applying shampoo so she doesn't wind up smelling like a frat house.

3. Use Cocktails as a Delivery Device

One of the main reasons women avoid beer is its reputation as a fattening drink. Granted, beer isn't the lowest-calorie beverage in the world. But you can always share this little fun fact with her: A twelve-ounce beer has fewer calories than a cosmopolitan.

Making cocktails with beer might feel a little like gilding the lily—no need to mess with beer's perfection—but what can you do? Some people just like cocktails. Keep your lady happy with a few recipes for beer cocktails:

Black and Satin

Mix equal parts dark ale or porter with champagne. If that's too fancy for you, go with a traditional black and tan—dark ale or porter with a light ale.

Mexican Iced Tea

Pour one and a half ounces of tequila and three ounces of beer (preferably Mexican) over ice. Garnish with lime.

Red-Eye

A beer Bloody Mary: Mix one part Clamato to two parts beer.

Shandy

Equal parts beer and lemonade equal happiness on a hot summer day. Replace the lemonade with alcoholic cider and it's a Snakebite.

The Depth Charge

Drop a shot of whiskey into a glass of beer and bottoms up! While it's probably not the right drink for changing hearts and minds about beer, it is a classic—pretty much every culture in the world has a version. A Jimmy and Guinney drops Jameson into Guinness. A Sake Bomb uses sake and a Japanese lager. In Korea, they plop soju into beer and call it a *Poktanju*.

The Rainbow Cone

This one is more of a mistake, one that I had the good fortune to live out. Actually, I was living out someone else's fantasy—

namely Diane Sawyer's. She and the rest of the cast of *Good Morning America* had taken career aptitude tests; Diane's suggested that she would be a great bartender. Which is what she was doing when I wandered into Hurley's, a bar around the corner from where I was performing in *Hairspray*. She asked me what I wanted. It seemed like it would be bad manners to endorse a single beer, so I endorsed them all. I told her to turn on all the taps and to run a pint glass right on down the line. The result: a Rainbow Cone. It was actually pretty good.

WEST COAST
BEER

"Show me the way to the next whiskey bar . . ."
—Jim Morrison (or Brecht/Weill,
for you purists out there)

 I quit Second City's touring company right after I married Bernadette. Not the best strategy for a guy embarking into holy matrimony with a woman and her two young children, but I caught a break: Not long after I left, Jim Belushi quit Second City's resident company, leaving a vacancy for a guy with the appropriate bone structure. They needed me. And I was glad to be back.

And guess what? I didn't suck anymore. Whether it was the time in the touring company, or just growing up, I was starting to develop my own voice.

But about a year later, in the fall of 1979, Bernadette got a call from NBC. They were shooting a pilot in Los Angeles for a primetime knockoff of *Saturday Night Live* called *The Show Must Go On*. Bernadette had big crazy hair in those days, and they thought she could bring a Gilda Radner–style energy to the show. She was getting a lot of attention from agents, producers, the networks—all of whom wanted her to move to L.A.

Bernadette and her (now *our*) kids moved west in a U-Haul van stuffed with all of our possessions. I stayed behind in Chicago to finish my contract at Second City, then pointed my green VW with the Rolls-Royce grille toward Los Angeles and drove out to join them.

HOW I REALLY LEARNED THE PERILS OF DRINKING AND DRIVING

Like I said earlier, we all knew drinking and driving was a bad idea, but until around 1980, when organizations like Mothers Against Drunk Driving began to make headway, there were still plenty of irresponsible guys—like me—who would do it anyway. Not for the thrill of driving under the influence, but because travel always seems more civilized when drinking is involved. Plus I could measure trips by the number of drinks that would be consumed along the way: "You want to go there? That's a two-beer ride."

I'm not a total cretin: While I'd occasionally drink and drive, I would never think of littering. That would be wrong. When I finished a beer, I winged it into the backseat. Every time I took a hard turn, all of the bottles and cans would jingle together like church bells.

Shortly after moving to L.A., I decided to get a California driver's license. I took the written test and turned it in to one of the DMV employees. "You passed," he said. "Now if you'll just get your car and pull it into Lane Four, we can get to the road test."

"Uh, my car?" I stammered. "I kind of assumed that there would be a state vehicle. . . ."

"No. Do you have a car here?"

"I'm going to need a minute." I ran to the VW, climbed in, and pulled up to the nearest Dumpster. I spent the next several minutes tossing bottles and cans out the moonroof into the trash. The car still smelled like a brewery, but despite a few odd looks, the clerk passed me anyway. I was so disturbed by the experience that I vowed never to drink in my car again.

||||||||||||||||||||||||||||||||||||||||||||||||||||||||||||||||||||||||||||||||||||||||||||||||||||||||||||||||||||||||||||||||||||

Bernadette's pilot wasn't picked up, but she scored another role in a pilot written and produced by Barry Levinson. He wasn't a famous director yet but had already spent ten years winning Emmys and Oscar nominations as a screenwriter. More than enough success to own a lovely house in the hills, filled with fabulous art, where he decided to throw the wrap party.

At the party, Bernadette and the rest of her ensemble cast were treated like stars. I was just the schlubby barnacle she'd carried on her back from Chicago. So I did a focus exercise that I do whenever I'm feeling insecure: I concentrated on the beer. Lucky me—not only was there plenty of beer, but it was a spread to end all spreads. Levinson was married in those days to writer Valerie Curtin, who could have made a career as a party hostess. The tables were lined with honey-baked hams and meat-carving stations. And in the middle of it all was a tray of hardboiled eggs, apparently hand-painted with elaborate designs.

It would have been rude not to try everything, so I did, working my way down the buffet line to the painted eggs. When I cracked one open, the odor took me by surprise—the egg smelled . . . *mature*. But what the hell did I know? Caviar doesn't smell so great either. I'd already opened it—it would be bad manners not to take a bite. And besides, I thought, *What if it's good?*

WHAT IF IT'S GOOD?

My friend Pete Goldfinger and I once visited a Chinese restaurant—highly rated by Zagat—on the South Side of Chicago, where I ate enough for twelve men. We'd just received the check, when it dawned on me that we'd forgotten to order the egg rolls, one of the reviewer's specific recommendations. "Well," I said, "I guess we're going to have to try the egg rolls."

Pete looked stunned. "But . . . but . . . we already ate!"

"I know, I know," I replied. "But what if it's good?"

Those simple words were more than just a rationalization to stuff my face with more food. They form the basis of my life's guiding philosophy, one that has led me to all sorts of unexpected places, especially when mixed with beer.

Even with a lot of help from a salt shaker, the egg tasted rotten, but I didn't let that stop me from finishing it. The impressive volume of beer I'd consumed before hitting the buffet line didn't do much to dampen my determination. I dropped the shell on a plate and headed off to find another beer to rinse out the taste. I'd just reached the bar when I heard a woman scream. It was Valerie, the hostess.

"Somebody ate one of my eggs!"

Valerie stared at my plate, a pile of gnawed bones, cigarette butts, and the fragments from the empty eggshell. Not just any eggshell, but the remnants of an *objet d'art*, hand-painted by some famous artist, that probably cost Valerie what I made in a year at Second City. Or what I would have made, if I still worked at Second City.

My head started to spin. Somewhere I could still hear Valerie wailing. "Who could have eaten one of these eggs? How could someone even think they were edible?"

Across the yard, another woman began to scream. Bernadette knew *exactly* who could have eaten one of those eggs.

Panic spread like the plague. I heard someone shout for paramedics. I suddenly felt so ill I was sure that I was going to die. So I ducked out of the beer line, snuck into the garden, and lay down on the ground. Better to die quietly than to torpedo Bernadette's career.

Incredibly, I survived. (How about our friend the eggshell? Nature's perfect container!) Bernadette's show, however, was not as lucky.

ROTTEN BEER

Did you know that ultraviolet light can cause isohumulones to decompose prematurely? Me neither, but apparently it's the secret behind skunk beer.

Isohumulones are chemical compounds that help to give beer its taste, including its bitterness. A little bitter is a good thing. But too much exposure to light, and the isohumulones produce a compound called MBT. The MBT, or what scientists call *skunky thiol*, makes beer taste very, very bad. How bad? The name skunky thiol wasn't chosen at random—it's pretty much identical to the chemical that skunks produce in their anal glands to frighten off predators.

Chalk one up to the brilliance of beer drinkers, or at least their taste buds, as it would have been impossible to come up with a name more descriptive than *skunk beer*, scientifically proven to taste literally like a skunk's ass.

Beer in kegs or cans generally doesn't see the light of day until you open one, but green or clear bottles are prime targets for skunkiness—you'll want to keep them stored in dark places.

It was a rocky start to our life in Los Angeles, but I'd learned my first lesson as a West Coaster: Not everything on the buffet table is for guests' consumption. No wonder people in L.A. are so skinny!

American Beer

Frank Zappa once said, "You can't be a real country unless you have a beer and an airline. It helps if you have some kind of a football team, or some nuclear weapons, but at the very least you need a beer." While America has had some pretty impressive football teams, numerous airlines, and weapons of mass destruction for a few decades, it took us a while to nail our beer requirement.

THE LOCAL BEER

These days no matter where you go you're likely to find a decent, locally-brewed craft beer. It's a far cry from the days of regional-ized distribution, when you couldn't take a trip to Colorado or Wisconsin without someone asking you to pick up some Coors or Leinenkugel.

I'm still a sucker for the old ways, even if most "regional" beers are just brand names wielded by multinational corporations. Wherever I go, I always try to make a point of enjoying the traditional "local" brew. This isn't a comprehensive list, but here are a few of my favorites:

Chicago	Old Style
Denver	Coors
Detroit	Stroh's
Minnesota	Cold Spring
New Orleans	Abita, Dixie
New York	Rheingold
Philadelphia	Yuengling (the oldest brewery in America!)
Pittsburgh	Iron City
Texas	Shiner Bock, Lone Star

For years, America suffered from a paradox: While beer is an essential part of our history, when it came to brewing tasty beers, our nation was more or less the laughingstock of the world.

How essential is beer to America? It's the reason the Pilgrims chose Plymouth Rock. "For we could not now take time for further search [to land our ship]," reads the *May-*

flower's log, "our victuals being much spent, especially our beer." Our nation's first president had his own recipe for brewing "small beer." And it was America, under God, that invented the beer can.

GEORGE WASHINGTON'S RECIPE "TO MAKE SMALL BEER"

No joke—you can find this 1757 recipe from our nation's Founding Father in one of his notebooks at the New York Public Library:

Take a large Siffer [Sifter] full of Bran Hops to your Taste. Boil these 3 hours then strain out 30 Gall[ons] into a cooler put in 3 Gall[ons] Molasses while the Beer is Scalding hot or rather draw the Melasses into the cooler & St[r]ain the Beer on it while boiling Hot. let this stand till it is little more than Blood warm then put in a quart of Yea[s]t if the Weather is very Cold cover it over with a Blank[et] & let it Work in the Cooler 24 hours then put it into the Cask—leave the bung open till it is almost don[e] Working—Bottle it that day Week it was Brewed.

Fortunately, America has recently undergone a second revolution, one that's helped us catch up to the rest of the world.

Like any revolution, it's hard to put your finger on the exact moment it began. It might have been the Anchor Brewery, which in the '70s began experimenting with beer-making techniques dating back to the California Gold Rush. It could have been the repeal of a law, in 1979, that prohibited people from brewing their own beer at home, energizing a new generation of pioneers. Or maybe people were just bored of drinking the same old light lagers. Whatever it was, the emergence of craft beers transformed America's beer industry, especially in California, although signs of the revolution were apparent across the country, all the way to Boston's Sam Adams.

WHAT'S IN A NAME?

One of the greatest things about American craft beers is the creativity its brewers show in naming their products. Here are a few of my favorite names:

Arrogant Bastard. A strong ale from the Stone Brewing Company in California.

Blithering Idiot Barleywine. An English-style brew produced by Pennsylvania's Weyerbacher Brewing Co.

Erin Go Braless. From Montana's Kettlehouse Brewery, which also produces a porter called Olde Bongwater.

Monkey Knife Fight. A spiced beer from Pennsylvania's Nodding Head Brewery.

Sweetwater Happy Ending Imperial Stout. The Sweetwater Brewing Company in Georgia also has beers called 420 Extra Pale Ale, Donkey Punch, and Ron Burgundy Scotch Ale.

Wasatch Polygamy Porter. From Utah, of course—their motto is "Why Drink Just One?"

CHEERS

SAM

What do you say, Norm?

NORM

Any cheap, tawdry thing that'll get me a beer.

 Instead of heading back to Chicago with our tails between our legs, Bernadette and I decided to give it a go in Los Angeles. I picked up small parts in episodes of *Soap* and *Hart to Hart* and played an exterminator on *Taxi,* hired by Danny DeVito's Louie De Palma to take down the world's biggest cockroach.

Then came a writers' strike that shut down the town and ushered in what Bernadette and I would come to call the Days of Generic Beer.

THERE IS NO SUCH THING
AS A BAD BEER

Some beer is expensive, and deservedly so. But a lot of the time it's hard to justify drinking the good stuff. So once you start giving up quality, how bad can it get? The good news is: not very.

Big beer companies are big because a lot of people like to drink their beer. Companies like Budweiser and Miller produce beers that taste good and are reasonably priced. But there are a lot of people—or, as the big beer companies would say, a significant segment of the marketplace—who are going to look past those reasonable prices and buy the cheapest beer in the store. Since the beer companies don't want to lose these customers, they cater to them: Bud makes Busch. Miller makes Meisterbrau and Milwaukee's Best.

Do the cheaper versions taste worse than the originals? Different, maybe, but it's not like the beer companies set out to make a beer that tastes subpar. They might take a few shortcuts with the ingredients, but most of the difference between the cheapies and the regulars is in the labeling. So to paraphrase old Father Flanagan of Boys Town, there is no such thing as a bad beer.

The strike ended after three months. And not long after, I caught a big break: a major supporting role in a new comedy. Soon people everywhere would know me as . . . Gus!

The show was called *Making the Grade*. I played Gus Bertoia, a superjock gym teacher at a high school in St. Louis. CBS picked up the pilot, written by a talented guy named Gary David Goldberg (who would go on to create *Family Ties* and *Spin City*), for a mid-season tryout. There would be no more generic beer for the family Wendt.

MY FAVORITE BEERS FOR A CELEBRATION

Pilsner Urquell on tap

Guinness, from a pub-draft can—the guys who invented that widget top really were brilliant

Pretty much any California craft-brewed IPA

In the midst of the excitement, I got a call from my agent. "George, honey, how are you, it's Jinny."

"I'm great! Really excited about the show. Gus is a perfect character for me. Maybe I'll actually get back into shape."

"That's wonderful, George, really wonderful. Listen,

honey, Jim Burrows called. He was wondering if you'd be available for a pilot he's directing for NBC. Something he's doing with the Charles brothers."

The Charles brothers—Glen and Les—were great comedy writers. They'd written the episode of *Taxi* I appeared in, which also happened to be directed by Jim Burrows. I was flattered that they wanted to work with me again. But.

"Jinny, I've already got a job."

"It's nothing, George, nothing. Just one line. One *word*. They really want you."

Now I really couldn't turn it down.

According to the original script, I wasn't supposed to appear until the end of the episode. By that time, one of the show's stars—played by another Second City alum, Shelley Long—has been dumped by her fiancée and taken a job as a waitress in a Boston bar. I was supposed to be George, her first customer. "I'm Diane," she would introduce herself. "I'll be your waitress." Then would come a rambling monologue, a minute long, about all of the strange circumstances that had led up to her becoming a waitress. My job was to look impatient, until Diane finally remembered she was talking to a thirsty customer. "Oh!" she'd exclaim. "I should take your order. What can I get you?"

At which point I was to deliver my single line. My single word, actually: "Beer."

"Beer, perfect!" she would reply, hurrying off to fill the order.

I had a lot of trouble believing that I was going to get

paid to look like a guy who really wanted a beer. Talk about a job that matched up with the real me. My passion must have shown through, because almost immediately, my role began to expand.

Sitcom scripts, especially pilots, are a fluid business. Until the actors are delivering lines—sometimes in front of a live studio audience—it's impossible to know which jokes are going to work and which lines are going to fall flat. The writers are always working on the fly. What begins as a fifty-page script on Monday might be fifty completely different pages on Friday.

By the end of the week in the bar, my character had a new entrance (I was the first regular customer to walk in) and a new point of view (I badgered Diane, rather than the other way around). I also had a new name: Norm Peterson.

And when *Making the Grade* got canceled after just six episodes, I was happy to have a new job waiting for me.

BAR TRIVIA

One of the actors who read for the part of George sensed that his audition hadn't gone well. With one foot out the door, he turned around and asked the producers if they had a character who was a know-it-all. "Every bar's got a know-it-all," he said.

He was right. Something about the combination of beer and social camaraderie drives people to get into arguments over obscure facts. The bar know-it-all is always at the center. He is, in fact, the reason world records were invented, even if the story sounds like something Monty Python might have whipped up. In the 1950s, a bar know-it-all named Sir Hugh Beaver got into a typical barroom debate over which was the fastest European game bird, the golden plover or the grouse. In a fit of beer-fueled inspiration, Beaver—who also happened to be the managing director of the Guinness Brewery—realized that know-it-alls needed a way to prove that they were right. The first *Guinness Book of World Records* was published a few years later.

The actor who suggested the idea to the *Cheers* producers proceeded to launch into an improvised monologue as the bar's know-it-all. John Ratzenberger was subsequently rewarded with the role of Cliff Clavin.

||||||||||||||||||||||||||||||||||||||||||||||||||||||||||||||||||||||||||||||||||||||||||||||||||||||||||||||||||||||||||||||||||||||||||||||||||||||||||||||||||||

Cheers premiered on NBC in 1982. Nobody noticed, except for a couple of critics. We finished the season in last place, 77th out of 77 primetime programs. The show aired Thursday nights, which at that time meant it was being crushed by CBS's unbeatable one-two: *Magnum, P.I.* and *Simon & Simon*.

We were lucky to have a lot of support from a boss who understood comedy. Back in my improv workshop days, before I made it into Second City, I used to help fold up the chairs after the more experienced students were done performing. One night one of my co-folders turned to me and said, "You know, George? That's going to be us up on that stage someday." He was half right. I made it. As for the co-folder, Brandon Tartikoff, he managed to do all right for himself. When *Cheers* began, he was the youngest-ever president of NBC's Entertainment Division and, more important, he had our backs.

A few more people watched the show when the CBS behemoths went to reruns. We got a big boost from the Emmys—five in our first season, the winners including Shelley Long, Jim Burrows for directing, and the Charles brothers for writing the pilot. And the one for Outstanding Comedy Series probably helped. Our ratings got a little better the second season, especially after NBC moved *Family Ties* to the slot before us. Then, in season three, the network added a new sitcom called *The Cosby Show*. It turned out to be the perfect lead-in to what became "Must See Thursday": *Cosby, Family Ties, Cheers, Night Court,* and *Hill Street Blues*.

NORM AND ME

One question I'm constantly asked is if I really like beer as much as Norm Peterson. "Nobody's *that* good of an actor," I tell them.

Despite the obvious similarities, however, there are a couple of critical differences between Norm and me. I actually like my wife; Norm, on the other hand, was a bit more ambivalent about his heard-but-never-seen wife, Vera (who, by the way, was voiced by Bernadette). And when I drink a lot of beer, I will occasionally get drunk. Not so for Norm: It was very important to the network (and to my mother) that Norm never seem like he was getting loaded. They didn't want him to appear pathetic.

But the biggest difference? Norm had *way* better writers than I do.

Bar Theory, Part One

People occasionally stop me on the street and ask, "Hey, are you Norm?"

"No," I reply. "But I played one on TV." It was a role I took seriously. So seriously, in fact, that you could say I've put in a lifetime of research.

And don't think I rest on my laurels. I like to keep my chops honed—the research never ends. Life on a barstool continues to teach me a few things along the way. Here's one.

How to Choose a Bar

Whoa! Slow down. Are you sure we need to go to a bar? Consider this scenario: Let's say you like to drink Heinekens. You can probably drink them at home for about a dollar a pop.

But if you go to a bar, you're probably going to have to pay $1.50 or more for the cheapest beer they serve. The bar, therefore, has to be good enough to justify paying more for less.

There are a lot of variables, of course, so you'll have to set up your own scoring system. Add points for the number of times you're likely to laugh, your chances of getting laid, and the number of available toilets. If you have to pass your house on the way to the bar, you're taking points off the board. Ditto if two of your friends are going to have to carry you home at three A.M.

A lot to remember, I know, but it's that important. I look forward to the day when some genius builds this into an iPhone application.

SOFTBALLS AND MOSCOW MALLS

"You know, you get bored going on a cross-
country flight Boston to L.A., so you gotta spend
the time doing something."
—Baseball Hall of Famer Wade Boggs, after
denying a rumor he once drank sixty-four beers
during a flight to the West Coast

 In 1959 the Chicago White Sox went to the World Series. It had been forty long, dry years since their last appearance, when they had intentionally lost the Series in the infamous Black Sox Scandal. Needless to say, the fans were ready to turn the page. The entire South Side of Chicago was buzzing with excitement. Especially our house. My dad, a lifelong fan, managed to score tickets to the first game of the Series, including a couple for my sister Kathy and me.

It was a day game, which meant that we'd have to miss

school to go. "Why don't we ask Sister Suzanne if it would be all right?" suggested my father.

Sister Suzanne, the principal of our grammar school, Christ the King, fit the classic mold—rigid and humorless. She didn't like to mince words, either. "Absolutely not!" she replied when we asked her if we could take the day off. We returned home, heads hung low, and told our father the bad news.

"Well," he declared, "some things are too important to be left up to the Church. This may be the only chance in your lifetime you'll get to see the World Series in Chicago." (He was almost right: The hapless Chicago Cubs have their "Billy Goat curse" that's kept them out of the World Series since 1945; the White Sox had the Curse of Mr. Wendt— they wouldn't play for another championship until 2005.)

The seats were right on the first-base line at the old Comiskey Park, a great place to watch the Sox crush the Dodgers eleven-zip, unless you were a hungry and thirsty kid. There weren't any vendors selling cotton candy, Cokes, or even hot dogs—just a tireless beer man peddling suds. Luckily, not only did Kathy and I think that "Beer, here!" was the most hilarious thing we'd ever heard—keeping us from dwelling on our empty stomachs and dry throats—but the beer man was a good sport, regaling us with stories about the good old days. I've connected sporting events with beer ever since.

BEST BALLPARK BEER

Any beer tastes great at a ball game, but Coors Field in Denver is the only baseball stadium that has its own on-site microbrewery. Fans can make their way down the right-field line to the Blue Moon Brewery at the Sandlot, where award-winning craft beers are served. Added bonus: You're at altitude. You may not catch a ball, but you'll probably catch a buzz.

My own baseball career was limited to a season in the minor leagues. By "minor leagues," I mean the Little League kind, where the plate is maybe forty feet from the pitcher's mound and no one's allowed to steal bases. I remember making contact exactly one time that year. The result: a foul ball. I was around second base by the time I realized they were calling me back to the plate. I sucked so badly at hitting that I once had a ball and strike called on the same pitch. "Ball!" yelled the umpire. That didn't stop me from swinging anyway, forcing the bewildered ump to amend his call. "Uh, strike?"

As is the case with so many childhood humiliations, I got the chance to relive my baseball failures as an adult. During a charity auction in Chicago, I bid on and won hitting lessons with then–White Sox slugger Frank Thomas. They weren't for me, but my kids, who got the chance to spend an afternoon at the old Comiskey Park, taking batting practice with the pros.

The session wound to a close, and the pros suggested that I take a turn at bat. "Suggested" probably isn't the right description, not when there are words like "teased," "taunted," and "shamed into" at our disposal. And it wasn't like my kids had to be encouraged to join in. So I stepped into the batter's box.

I managed to foul off the first pitch, bringing back a flood of childhood memories. The most vivid was the reminder that unless you hit the ball square in the sweet spot of the bat, it's going to feel like a swarm of pissed-off bees are stinging your hands. I howled in pain.

The next ten pitches went more or less the same way. I sounded like Morris the Cat: "OW, ow, ow, ow. OW, ow, ow, ow. OW, OW, ow, ow, OW, ow, ow, ow!" Until finally, a miracle: I somehow managed to get all of one. I mean, all of my power, all of my weight, driving the ball as hard as I could toward the fences. I remember standing proudly at the plate, tracing the ball's majestic flight.

The feeling didn't last very long. The ball landed with a soft thud a couple of feet past the infield. I looked over toward the dugout to see my kids laughing at me, Frank Thomas laughing at me, and half of my beloved White Sox franchise laughing at me. My hands didn't hurt, but my pride had taken another beating.

Softball is an entirely different story. Unless you're a total diehard, you can pretty much replace the words "softball game" with "drunken gathering" without losing too much of any story. That doesn't mean I actually play softball. Not anymore, anyway. I imagine myself slapping the ball into left field, taking two steps toward first, and hearing *blam, blam!* as onlookers duck to avoid what sounds like gunfire. Relax, folks: Those were just my Achilles tendons exploding. But softball did get my picture into *Sports Illustrated* (with a mighty assist, of course, from my love of beer).

Sometime in March 1989, I found myself drinking in San Francisco's Washington Square Bar and Grill. For those of you who don't remember the Washbag, as it was affectionately nicknamed by the legendary *San Francisco Chronicle* columnist and regular Washbag customer Herb Caen, it was the kind of place that catered to literate geezers—not just newspapermen, but college professors, city politicians, and patrons of the arts. And like every good neighborhood bar, the Washbag had its own softball team.

The average player was in his mid-fifties. Herb Caen manned first base well into his seventies. None of which stood in the way of the team's ambitions. In 1979, the bar's colorful proprietor, Ed Moose, pointed out that in order to be a legitimate franchise, they had to play at least one game on the road. So a road game was scheduled . . . in Paris, France. Stoked by their brutal domination over those French dandies (the score was either 40–22 or 40–20—the scorekeeper apparently lost track), this motley band of geezers adopted a new name: *Les Lapins Sauvages*. They'd been aiming for a pun—"the Wild Hares"—but their pedestrian French actually translated to "the Wild Rabbits," a name that's stuck ever since. In the years that followed, the Lapins went on to play road games in London, Dublin, and Hong Kong.

Back to 1989, where I was rising from the bar to call for a taxi. I couldn't help but notice a flyer on the wall advertising the Lapins' next contest: *High Noon! Mother's Day! Moscow!* Keep in mind that this was the pre-collapse, *Rocky IV* Soviet Union: The Iron Curtain was still very much intact, guarded by stone-faced generals with outrageous eyebrows. "Is this for real?" I asked Ed Moose.

"Sure is," he replied. "The first softball game ever played in the USSR."

"You know," I said, "I might be in Moscow around then." By sheer coincidence, I'd just been hired to play the title character in a BBC television adaptation of *Oblomov*, a nineteenth-century Russian satire about a useless nobleman who doesn't even get out of bed for the first 150 pages of the book (the word *Oblomovshchina* is still used by Russians to mean "incredible sloth"). The Brits had updated the story to the modern day—I was a slothful bureaucrat instead of a slothful nobleman—and had somehow secured the rights to shoot on location in the Soviet Union.

"If you're going to be there, why don't you come play with us?" Ed suggested.

"Uh, probably not. But I'd love to come and drink a few beers. Where's the game?"

"Dunno."

The location was still T.B.D., which didn't bode well for

my chances of hooking up with the Wild Rabbits: It was the
'80s, after all, and we were years away from cell phones,
emails, and text messages. Still, I filed the game away in the
back of my mind.

Maybe Russians will tell you otherwise, but from my
point of view, 1989 wasn't a great time to be a Russian.
Today's Moscow is cosmopolitan, with gourmet restaurants,
a Ritz-Carlton, and a damn good beer, Baltika. But back
then, the food was awful. The only safe thing to eat was the
appetizers, and even then only things that had been smoked
or preserved. Main courses were a gamble, both to your pal-
ate and your health—suffice it to say that "fresh" doesn't
mean the same thing everywhere in the world. (Rare indeed
was the green vegetable that wasn't a wilting cucumber.)
Beer was even rarer—any store that had it also had a long
line of thirsty customers who guzzled the half-liter bottles
as soon as they'd paid for them.

No, it wasn't a great time to be a Russian. But we weren't
Russians; we were the British Broadcasting Corporation.

The BBC could get to places that tourists—not to mention most locals—could not. The cast and crew were issued
work visas, giving us a sort of all-access, backstage pass to
the city. That, plus the fact that we were carrying dollars
and pounds instead of rubles, allowed us to shop at food
halls that could have given Harrods a run for its money.
More important, it gave us access to beer, a not-unimportant
detail given that this was predominantly a British crew.

The one trip we took outside of Moscow was an overnight train ride to Kostroma, a historic city along the Upper Volga River. The small crew, maybe a half-dozen people, wheeled an equipment trolley aboard the train. About a third of it was loaded with the camera equipment; the rest was stacked with beer. That trolley was followed by two more trolleys, each one stocked entirely with beer. I am still in awe of the crew's daily regime: They worked like dogs all day, then drank and played cards all night. I don't know that any of them ever slept. Truly amazing beer drinkers, the British.

We turned out to have a break in the schedule during Mother's Day weekend, so I decided to seek out Les Lapins Sauvages. What might have seemed like an impossible task was made simpler by the restrictive Soviet government: Since Ed and his crew were tourists, there were only three or four hotels where they could possibly be staying. The hardest part about finding them turned out to be hailing a cab.

Interesting factoid about cabdrivers in a Communist society: They get paid the same whether they pick up fares or not. I figured this out when I raised my hand, hoping to catch the attention of a group of cabbies smoking cigarettes near their parked taxis. They saw me, but no one looked very eager to drive me anywhere. Fortunately, I had a pack of Marlboros. I held it up long enough for one of the drivers to show a tiny bit of interest. That was just the beginning of the negotiation. His enthusiasm seemed to take a hit when we established that we weren't talking American dollars or even rubles for the fare—I only wanted to spend a few kopecks—but he stayed on the line long enough for us to negotiate a price. We settled on ten rubles and a pack of Marlboros, sparing us both the indignity of taking off my shoes and socks, and set out for the Kosmos, the nearest hotel that catered to tourists.

I knew I was in the right place as soon as I walked into the lobby, thanks to the singing that floated in from the bar—a group rendition of "Take Me Out to the Ball Game." The Lapins were happy to see a familiar face. Ed Moose had even gone through the trouble of making a jersey for me. We drank together for hours.

"So when's the game tomorrow?" I finally thought to ask.

As close as I'd ever get to the Big Leagues.

"High Noon!" Ed said.

"Have you figured out where?"

"Young Pioneers of the Republic Park."

"See you there!"

The next morning, I had the good sense to request a driver from the BBC—no more messing around with taxis. The driver arrived while I was brushing my teeth. "Where are we going?" he asked.

I spit the toothpaste from my mouth. "A place called the Young Pioneers of the Republic Park. Do you know it?"

"Sure," the driver said, smiling. "Which one?"

"What do you mean, 'which one'? How many are there?"

He shrugged his shoulders. "Maybe a couple of thousand?"

As it turns out, every kid born in the USSR was a Young Pioneer of the Republic. The name was more or less synonymous with "Children's Park."

"Listen," I told the driver, "I'm not going to waste your day going to every park in the city. But maybe while I get dressed, you could check out the one nearest to the Hotel Kosmos? Tell me if there are any men in funny-looking outfits."

The driver looked at me strangely but agreed. He returned a short time later. "Is the place," he said.

It was obvious why as soon as we got there. A thousand people had shown up to see the game. Both CNN and Soviet television stations sent camera crews. The two teams exchanged gifts in an extravagant ceremony.

The game itself was slightly less entertaining than *Rocky IV*. With the Lapins ahead 12–0, someone suggested that the lead was probably safe enough for me to play. As I trotted out to man right field for an inning, a photographer from *Sports Illustrated* snapped my picture.

Final score: Lapins 18, Ruskies 4. But there weren't any of the bad feelings you'd normally associate with a blowout—the mood after the game was closer to jubilation. We all returned to the bar at the Kosmos—players, diplomats, and television crews—where we drank beer and sang into the early hours of the morning. I spent the rest of the night making new friends and trying to guess whether they were CIA or KGB. Or both.

Beer
and
Fitness

I have been lucky: I have not had to move very much in my life. I live in an age of automobiles. I don't suffer any great urge to push it to the limit, work on my core, or engage in acts of extreme fitness. Much of my acting career has taken place on a barstool. When Jim Burrows used to give me direction on *Cheers*, it was mainly to shift my ass around so that I wouldn't obstruct the camera's view of Ted Danson. "Left cheek, Georgie," Jim would say. "Okay, Georgie, now the right cheek."

As a result, I am extremely low mileage at sixty. I feel like I have plenty left in the tank, the ligaments of a forty-year-old. I credit my philosophy of Minimal Movement: Why run when you can walk? And why walk at all?

I've always thought life would be easier on a barstool. You know, one that moved. I could be like Lionel Barrymore in his wheelchair. Directors could work around me, blocking every scene in a way that allowed me to sit down. "Well, if I'm over here, on this stool, it's a good way to show my emotions."

"But your character is supposed to be angry . . ."

"Haven't you ever heard of passive aggression?"

BARSTOOL WORKOUT

Working hard and playing hard don't have to be mutually exclusive. Take exercise, for example. Over the years, I've developed a few methods for sneaking in my workout without interfering with Happy Hour. Here are a few:

Speak loudly—bellowing engages the abdominal muscles.

Try to order your beer in a mug—liter-sized, if they've got one. A couple of hours of raising and lowering a full mug of beer and you'll give your biceps a workout they won't soon forget.

If your watering hole has barstools, try to find the one that needs a book of matches to level it out. It'll force you to rock back and forth, "working your core" the entire time.

Standing at a bar and feeling supermotivated? I've got two words for you: ass clenches.

Don't be afraid to stagger. It's simple geometry: Drunken zigzagging can transform getting from Point A to Point B into a minimarathon.

Finally, as a closing note, be kind to your trainer. If you're going to be drinking a lot, think about moving closer to the tap—the bartender's actually working, not working out.

It probably won't come as any surprise that the fastest I've ever moved in my life was in pursuit of beer.

Shortly after college, I took a trip to Jamaica with a few friends: Joe Farmar, Mike McDonald, and Cynthia Cavalenes, a stage manager from Second City. It was an escape from the pressures of our regular lives, free of any stress, except for one: The stores that sold beer were closed on Sundays.

We knew we needed a plan, so we came up with one: At 4:45 Saturday afternoon, fifteen minutes before the stores closed for the evening, we sent Mike down the hill to stock up on beer. The rest of us went about our normal business, which was standing in a pool up to our necks, taking in the sunshine.

A few minutes later, Mike returned to the pool with two six-packs. We each popped open a brew and took a long sip. "So how much did you get?" I asked.

"What do you mean, 'how much did I get'?" Mike replied. "You're looking at it."

"Wait a minute," Joe said. "Are you saying that we only have another eight beers to get us to Monday? For four of us?"

It shouldn't have been a surprise—Mike had a well-deserved reputation for being cheap. What was more surprising was how fast we sprung into action. Joe and I shot out of the pool like Polaris missiles, sprinted down the hill like jackrabbits, and made it to the store just before closing time.

Nowadays, I'm smarter than that. When I get up to go to the fridge, I'll grab two or three beers. That way I don't have to stress about finishing one on the way back to the chair.

Believe it or not, I used to be a gym rat and a halfway decent basketball player. I was also half my current weight. Fortunately, getting slower hasn't ruined my game: It's just allowed it to mature.

While overweight players tend to get drummed (or drumsticked) out of the NBA, almost every recreational basketball player has, at some time or another, run into what I'll call the fat man's game. For the non–basketball inclined, the fat man's game revolves around accentuating the positive—in this case, his weight—and using this advantage to knock over his defender, clearing the space the fat man needs to fling a skyhook or a one-handed set shot toward the basket. The ability to shoot with one hand is especially important, as it frees the fat man's other hand for a beer (and, under ideal conditions, food).

You might be able to defend yourself against this style of play, but you won't want to. Simple physics dictate that there's going to be a lot of body contact: bigger guy, more surface area. And while you may win, you're going home wearing the fat man's perspiration. Even worse, there's no upside. No one's impressed when you block his shot. But when a guy whose vertical leap is measurable not in inches but in sheets of looseleaf paper somehow manages to blow by you, you just know you're not going to live that one down anytime soon.

Before you go cursing the fat man's game, try walking a mile in my shoes. Or, better yet, try playing a game with a nineteen-inch television set—I'm talking the old school box with picture tubes, not a flat-screen—duct-taped to your belly. See if you don't use your weight to knock people over. Is it illegal? Maybe. But you don't hear me complaining when you, you know, *run*.

BARS

"We have to recognise, that the gin-palace, like
many other evils, although a poisonous, is still
a natural outgrowth of our social conditions.
The tap-room in many cases is the poor man's
only parlour. Many a man takes to beer, not
from the love of beer, but from a natural
craving for the light, warmth, company, and
comfort which is thrown in along with the beer,
and which he cannot get excepting by buying
beer. Reformers will never get rid of the drink
shop until they can outbid it in the subsidiary
attractions which it offers to its customers."
—William Booth,
founder of the Salvation Army

"Was I in here last night and did I spend a
twenty dollar bill? What a load that is
off my mind! I thought I'd lost it!"
—Egbert Sousé (W.C. Fields)
in *The Bank Dick*

 In 1993—as *Cheers* was coming to an end—I landed a role in *Wild Men*, a play written by some old Second City pals, including my friend Pete Burns. The role was a real stretch for me: I played an alcoholic commodities trader who makes his stage entrance holding a can of Budweiser in each hand. Essentially I was Norm's evil twin.

After opening in Chicago, the play moved to New York City. The Westside Theatre was in the heart of Hell's Kitchen, a neighborhood that wasn't quite as bad as the name might suggest but wasn't exactly known for its glamorous nightlife at the time. That didn't stop Pete and me from sampling most of the bars in the area.

We'd surmised from Page Six—the *New York Post*'s daily gossip column—that the beautiful people all favored the downtown scene, so we decided to check it out for ourselves. But the supposedly trendy Lower East Side bar we chose turned out to be dead. We asked the bartender if he could recommend a livelier place where we'd at least have a chance of spotting a movie star or a supermodel. Even a regular model. "I hear everybody's going to Club U.S.A. in Times Square," he offered. We dropped a tip in his jar and caught a cab uptown.

True to the bartender's word, the scene at Club U.S.A. was hopping. The taxi stopped in front of velvet ropes and a line that extended around the block. I elbowed Pete. "Definitely supermodels." The night got even more exciting when I got out of the cab. The doorman recognized me from

Cheers. The ropes parted, sucking Pete and me into a dark club with pulsating music. *Thumpa! Thumpa! Thumpa! Thumpa!* Guys in jockstraps danced in cages hung from the ceiling. "New York!" I shouted to Pete. "Kinky!"

I should note here that Pete is a pretty good-looking guy. Hunky, you might say. So it wasn't surprising that he attracted a lot of attention. As we moved deeper into the dark labyrinth, it was almost like people were following us. Mostly men, I noticed. As my eyes grew accustomed to the dark, I realized that Pete's followers were *only* men, many of whom were dressed in Li'l Abner overalls with one strap undone and no shirt underneath.

In the years since my foray into Club U.S.A., I've enjoyed a lot more exposure to all kinds of lifestyles. I played a woman, Edna Turnblad, in *Hairspray*, and dressed as one through most of another play, *Minsky's*. But at the time, I was much more of a typical Midwesterner who'd spent half his life in Jesuit schools, an "aw shucks" farmboy on a trip to the big city. "Pete," I said, "we've got to get out of here."

"Why?" he said. "I kind of like this place."

"I think it's a gay bar," I whispered.

Pete's eyes darted around the room. Several men seemed to be eyeing him like wolves around a lost sheep. We backed slowly out of the bar, not stopping until we were at the entrance. "Is there something we should know about this bar?" I asked the doorman.

The doorman just shrugged. "Sunday night. Club U.S. *Gay.*"

The Wendt sisters get ready for a night on the town.

Pete and I had a good laugh. We were still laughing the next day when we read about our visit in Page Six: One of their tipsters reported seeing George Wendt and his "unidentified male companion" at Club U.S. Gay.

Sometimes, as the song goes, you want to go where everybody knows your name. Sometimes you don't. I was in the latter kind of mood once during a trip to Dublin, Ireland, and asked my friend Vinny, a local, to recommend a bar where no one would care that I was on TV. He suggested a place called the Ferryman.

When we arrived, the Ferryman was empty, or nearly so—the only other customers were a couple chatting quietly in the back of the bar. We ordered beers and Vinny excused himself to go to the bathroom. That's when the lady half of the couple approached me. "My friend would really like to meet you," she said. So much for keeping a low profile.

I followed her to the back of the bar, ready to shake hands with a fan. Only when we arrived at her table, I was the one who was star-struck—her friend turned out to be Bono. "Hello," he said in that unmistakable Irish brogue. "I didn't want to meet you because you were Norm from *Cheers*. I wanted to meet you because you were Norm from *Cheers* and you found *this* place. Dublin's in sort of a code, and you've cracked it!" We wound up drinking together for the next couple of hours.

I dined out on this story for years, sometimes literally: One night I told it to Woody Harrelson and Jim Burrows over dinner, on our way to a U2 concert at the Staples Center in downtown L.A. They treated my tale with the kind of "no shit?" skepticism that I've received from most of the people I've told over the years. No one thinks I'm lying, exactly; they just kind of assume that what for me was an unforgettable experience was a passing blip on the radar for a legend like Bono.

Woody had scored backstage passes, so when we arrived at the arena we were ushered into the quote-unquote "VIP section." Most of the time these passes are bullshit: The band stays sequestered in some secret back-backstage, while all the people with backstage passes are herded into a crowded room with lukewarm beer and picked-over cheese platters.

Only this time, I actually saw U2's guitarist, The Edge,

standing on the other side of the room. A minute later, I felt a tap on my shoulder. I turned around to see Bono.

"Hello," he greeted me. "I don't know if you remember me, but we met once at a pub in Dublin."

FIVE GOOD BAR BETS

Bar bets may have been responsible for some of Shakespeare's plays and possibly Scientology. They're certainly responsible for a midnight baseball game played every year in Anchorage. But mostly bar bets are about free beer. We like free beer. Here are five field-tested ways to score a free pint.

1. Groucho's Mirror. Ever see that old Marx Brothers skit where Harpo pretends to be Groucho's mirror reflection? This one works the same way. Pick a mark and bet that he can't mimic everything you do for sixty seconds.

Start slow, maybe moving your glass a foot to the right. Touch your finger to your nose. Spin a lighter. Tap a simple rhythm on the table. Take a sip of your beer and make an exaggerated show of swallowing it. Then, as sixty seconds approaches, take another sip of beer and *pretend* to swallow it. The idea is that the other guy won't know you're pretending and will go ahead and swallow the beer. Your next move: Spit the beer in your mouth back into your glass. Checkmate.

2. Super-Chugger. Bet the mark that you can down three full pints of beer before he can finish a single shot. All you ask are two things: first, that he gives you a head start, allowing you a one-beer lead to lubricate your throat; and second, that he at no time touches any of your beer glasses, as you don't want him messing with your rhythm.

Once he agrees to the bet, drink the first pint and, when finished, place it facedown over the shot glass. As he's agreed not to touch your glass, he's going to have to watch helplessly as you take your time finishing the other two pints.

3. The Polish Mentalist. No, it isn't exactly politically correct, but it's still damn funny. Grab a pen and cocktail napkin and ask someone in your party to choose a number between one and ten thousand. Tell them not to disclose it but to concentrate on the number in order to facilitate the telepathic connection the two of you are about to share. Act as if you're writing the number down on the napkin, then guess aloud: "Is your number . . . 703?"

You don't have to choose 703; any number will do. What's important is that nine thousand nine hundred and ninety-nine times out of ten thousand, they'll answer "No." At which point you can show them the cocktail napkin, on which you've already written "No!" (By the way, if you somehow happen to guess the number right, you can just crumple up the napkin and throw it away. It's a no-lose proposition!)

4. The Swami. Ask the mark to hold a penny in one hand and a nickel in the other without showing you which—you're going to use your psychic powers to figure it out.

Tell her to multiply the value of the coin in her right hand by two without saying the answer out loud. Then tell her to multiply the value of the coin in her left hand by sixteen, again keeping her answer to herself.

The trick is the amount of time it takes her to make the second calculation. If she figures it out quickly, she's probably holding the penny in her left hand—it doesn't take most people very long to multiply sixteen by one. If it takes her a few seconds (or more), she's probably trying to multiply sixteen by five, which means the nickel is in her left hand.

5. The Flashing Bartender. This one involves a little preparation but is generally worth it, as it succeeds most of the time. Pull a twenty-dollar bill (or higher, if your friends are flush) out of your wallet and announce: "I've got a twenty-dollar bill right here that says the bartender is going to pull up her shirt and show us her breasts."

When you get a taker, simply show him the twenty-dollar bill you're holding, on which you've already written: "The bartender is going to pull up her shirt and show us her breasts."

Bar Theory, Part Two

Here are a few more professional-grade tips to enhance your bar-going pleasure:

Have a Plan

You should approach a bar—especially a crowded one—the way the Allies planned for Normandy. Whoever's ordering should create a beachhead. The rest of your party can be arranged into supply lines—use runners if there's room, or conveyance routes if the place is packed.

Pick Your Team Carefully

Choose appropriate drinking companions—you never know when you're going to need a friend or two to help you find

My dad (an ideal drinking companion) and me on the set of *Cheers*.

your way home. I'll drink with just about anyone, as long as he or she can abide by my one basic rule: Don't totally humiliate yourself.

Know Your Weaknesses

If you're of a certain age, don't be afraid to play "the old card." When I walk into a crowded bar, I'll usually suss out a strapping young man on a barstool. "Dude, I've got to sit," I'll say to him. "Do you think I could borrow your seat for five minutes?" Nine times out of ten it's all yours.

Never Surrender at the First Sign of Trouble

Finally, Thou Shalt Avoid Breaking the Seal. At some point you're probably going to have to pee. Just don't give in to your first impulse: Once the seal is broken, there's no closing that door—you'll be making trips to the head for the rest of the night. Ignore the first call. You'll get a more urgent one in about an hour or so.

BEER
AND GOLF

"If you drink, don't drive. Don't even putt."
—Dean Martin

 My father was an avid golfer, and like any father who's avid about anything, he dreamed of the day I'd follow in his cleats. There's a lot to like about golf, namely its relationship to beer. I mean, you could probably convince me to take a spinning class if there was a drinks cart involved.

But golf also means mornings. If you're a beer drinker, mornings are a problem. For example, where exactly are you going to poop?

Then there's the whole problem of the sun. I hate the sun. I'll confess that some of this hatred is a byproduct of my theatrical training. Theater people are the world's ultimate second-shifters. Nothing happens in their universe before four o'clock. The workday might end at midnight. A couple of beers after the show, and—whoa, look at the time—it's three A.M.! A few beers more, and you're liable to see the sunrise. Now I know there are plenty of people who associate daybreak with rebirth and renewal: a fresh start. Those people haven't been up drinking all night. I tend to associate the morning sun with the feeling of a ball-peen hammer driving an exclamation point into my skull.

The rest of my dislike comes from my physical makeup. Fat people, as a rule, do not do well with heat. But I'm also the son of a redheaded woman of Irish descent which presents me with the added misfortune of having fair skin. In other words, the more intense the sunlight, the more I've got to wrap myself up like the Unabomber. Which only exacerbates the part about the heat. *Follow the shade*, is what I say. (Yes, this is a book about beer *and* skincare.)

Therefore, my experience with golf has been bittersweet. On the plus side, as I noted earlier, there's the drinks cart, but the harsh conditions, coupled with the fact that I suck at the game, leave me at best feeling strongly ambivalent.

That being said, I will golf. I have golfed. From time to time I'll show up at charity tournaments, where I will suck at golf in public. You know, for the kids. But I don't enjoy it. I'd much rather just buy a box of balls, toss them in the lake, and spend the rest of the afternoon riding around in the cart drinking beer.

Sometimes I'm asked to do personal appearances, usually for charities or corporate events. They're basically assembly lines where I shake hands with somebody, toast the camera for a picture, and move on to the next attendee. I call these appearances "Norm Petting Zoos." I love this work. I get to meet people and drink beer and occasionally even get paid for it.

The best personal appearance I ever did was for Gateway computers. The company held a charity golf tournament near their corporate headquarters in North Sioux City, South Dakota. I was greeted warmly by the event's organizers. "Great to have you, George. We were thinking that you'd do your comedy routine, maybe twenty-five minutes or so, at the banquet after the tournament. What do you say?"

"Comedy routine?" I stammered. "Uh, I don't exactly have an act."

"Okay, no act. Maybe you could play golf with some of the employees? You could be part of a foursome with our top sellers."

"Golf, right. You want this to be *fun*, don't you?" I asked. Then an idea popped into my head: "What if I drove the beer cart?"

"The beer cart? We've already hired a spokesmodel to do that."

"Even better. I'll ride shotgun. That way I won't have to drink and drive."

The morning of the tournament, every player got a package that included a box of balls, a commemorative shirt, and a disposable camera. They didn't know what the camera was for until a beautiful woman drove up in a golf cart with beers and, of course, that Norm guy. Very successful event!

My least successful golfing experience didn't involve any clubs, although I wish that it had.

I was in Orlando, Florida, on a shoot, and the production company decided to put me up in a bungalow at a golf resort. I found myself with a day off and figured I'd get some exercise. I've often heard the game described as "a long walk spoiled," so I decided to skip the bad parts and stick to walking the course.

The grass was soggy so I kept on the cart paths. It's really kind of amazing how beautiful some golf courses can be when people aren't tearing divots into them with little white balls. I came upon a pond, shimmering in the sunlight, with three of the most graceful swans I'd ever seen floating on the surface. *See that?* I said to myself. *If I were golfing, I wouldn't have seen the beautiful pond or the magic of nature—I would have seen a water hazard.*

As I got nearer to the water, one of the swans came out to greet me. I felt like Dr. Doolittle. "Hey there, big fella," I said, holding out my hands in the universal gesture of peaceful relations. "You sure are pretty."

To which the swan replied, "YAAAAAACK!"

"Bad mood, huh? Maybe I've got a snack. . . ." I began digging through my pockets for food. When I looked up, I saw that the swan was closing distance on me. Quickly, and with what appeared to be extreme malice. "Boo!" I yelled, figuring I'd scare the bird away.

Instead, the swan extended its ten-foot wings and three-foot-long neck, looking a lot more like an angry Velociraptor than any daffy duck. It unleashed a bloodcurdling cry that sent fear up my spine. "Okay," I tried to reason with it. "How about you go your way, and I'll go mine." My way, I decided, was behind me. I began to back up slowly . . . right into the side of a hill. I tumbled backward onto the ground like a sorority sister getting chased in a horror movie.

The swan moved a lot faster than any movie monster. In an instant, it was on top of me. *Holy shit*, I realized. *I'm fighting for my life with a giant duck.* The bird was doing everything in its power to bite me. I wasn't sure if the beak could do any serious damage, but I wasn't of a mind to find out. I shielded my face with my hands, writhing back and forth on the ground to avoid the swan's bobbing head. *Think fast, George . . . you're going to lose this fight.*

My hands and chest were occupied, but I still had my legs. I wrapped them around the swan's body in a scissors-hold, squeezed as hard as I could, twisted sharply, and slammed the beast to the ground with a satisfying thud.

For a couple of seconds, the swan didn't move. I thought I'd killed the poor bird, until it staggered to its feet and began squawking at me again, this time with a little less bravado. I squawked back, collecting the cell phone and wallet that had fallen out of my pockets, and made a beeline for the pro shop.

"This is crazy!" I stormed into the store. "I was just attacked by one of your swans!"

The shop's clerk didn't look surprised. "Uh huh." He nodded. "Those are three mean swans."

"Mean? Honestly, if I'd had a golf club I would have beaten him in the head!"

"Can't say I blame you."

"Does this kind of thing happen often?"

"Oh yeah. All the time."

"All the time?"

"Sure," he said. "There used to be four swans."

I immediately set off to find the drinks cart.

BEER
AND FAITH

"Beer is proof that God loves us
and wants us to be happy."
—Benjamin Franklin, although arguably a
misquotation: he may have been talking
about wine. Either way, he's right.

My friend Pat gives up beer every year for Lent. Not all beer, just a *type* of beer. Some years that means draft. When he really wants to punish himself, he gives up bottles and cans. "You know how many places don't serve draft?" Pat will grumble, usually as he's ordering a margarita.

Depending on your point of view, you might think Pat's behavior sounds funny. Or sad. In truth, he's honoring a centuries-old monastic tradition. Lent is actually a big part of the reason beer tastes so good in the first place.

Early European monks were supposed to fast during

Lent, which meant no solid food. But no one said anything about beverages. Enter beer, or as the monks called it, "liquid bread." Believe it or not, they weren't just looking for an excuse to slap on a buzz—the monks considered beer to be a health food. "In wine there is wisdom, in beer there is strength," began an old German proverb. "In water, there is bacteria."

Laughable, right? Maybe, but consider the facts. The ancient Jews thought beer was so pure that it was inherently kosher. In its natural state, beer has no fat, no cholesterol, no caffeine, and no nitrates. It has a little protein, plenty of carbohydrates, lots of vitamin B, and important trace minerals like magnesium and potassium. Despite being more than 90 percent water, an average beer has about 150 calories, meaning that a few beers are more than enough to keep the body going when solid food isn't an option.

The monks brewed their own beer and shared it with travelers and guests—monasteries were the original Holiday Inns of their day. Word of this holiest of beverages quickly spread. Fortunately, many of these monasteries were located on rivers, making distribution as easy as loading a boat. And before too long, nearly all of Europe was going crazy for beer. Talk about doing the Lord's work!

|||||||||||||||||||||||||||||||||||||||||||||||||||||||||||||||||||||||||||||||||||||||||||||||||||||||||||||||||||||

PATRON SAINTS OF BEER

|||||||||||||||||||||||||||||||||||||||||||||||||||||||||||||||||||||||||||||||||||||||||||||||||||||||||||||||||||||

You might be disappointed to learn, as I did, that there was no real-life St. Pauli Girl—the beer took its name from a monastery whose monks served St. Paul. But beer has been associated with all that is holy for over a thousand years, producing dozens of religious heroes. St. Arnold of Metz warned people about the bacteria in water, suggesting they drink beer instead. St. Brigid is supposed to have transformed her bathwater into beer, feeding a colony of hungry lepers. But when it comes to beer's patron saints, here are the big four:

St. Luke the Evangelist

Born in Greece at the start of the first century A.D., Luke was an early physician, which made him a natural patron saint to doctors and butchers alike. His fondness for scientific experimentation was also an inspiration to brewers, many of whom considered him the first patron saint of beer.

St. Nicholas of Myra

A Turkish bishop who lived around the turn of the fourth century, he was rumored to have resurrected three unlucky travelers who had been murdered and turned into meatpies by an evil innkeeper. (*Sweeney Todd* this!) His reputation as a protector of hotel guests soon extended to all visitors of inns, especially those who came in to toss back a few. Today, however, St. Nick is better known for his anonymous acts of charity and the German bastardization of his name, "Santa Claus."

St. Augustine of Hippo

He was one of the most important thinkers in Church history, the brains behind concepts like original sin, just war, and the style of corporeal punishment that is still practiced today in Catholic schools around the world. But before he became a part of the establishment, St. Augustine had a reputation as a wild child, worshiping pagan gods and consorting with concubines. His eventual conversion to a life of moderation (as opposed to straight-up denial) was an inspiration to brewers and beer drinkers everywhere, who considered him a patron saint.

St. Wenceslaus, Duke of Bohemia

"Good King Wenceslaus," as he's known from the song, brought Christianity to the Czech peoples. As a ruler he was wildly adored, thanks in large part to his defense of his land (then called "Bohemia") and its greatest natural resource: hops. By the tenth century, the Bohemian hops used to make beer had become so popular that imitators often tried to sneak cuttings out of the country in order to replant them elsewhere. Wenceslaus put an end to the practice by instituting the death penalty for anyone caught smuggling hops over the border.

Interestingly enough, a second King Wenceslaus, who ruled over the region in the thirteenth century, carried on the tradition of his namesake by convincing the Pope to reconsider an order banning the production of beer.

My mother is very fond of the Catholic Church, specifically the clergy. And the clergymen love my mother. At times my house has been a sort of salon for the local priesthood, a place for good meals, conversation, and drink. Occasionally a clergyman even spends the night.

Before you get any ideas, let me assure you that there was no sexual component to any of these visits. I'm not saying that those sorts of things don't happen—my friend Joe Farmar can tell you about the time a priest challenged him to improve his grades by way of a naked wrestling match—but they never happened under my roof, where the only sin was occasional gluttony.

One night, while I was still in college, my friend Mike McDonald came to visit. After we'd worked through most of the beer in the fridge, my mother suggested that he spend the night in our guestroom. Mike climbed into bed, but he couldn't sleep, thanks to the loud snoring coming from the other side of the room.

"George," he yelled. "Shut up, will you?"

Snore.

"George, you sound like a goddamn chainsaw. Wake up, will you?"

When that didn't work, Mike threw his shoe, which banged noisily off the wall but didn't do a thing about the snoring. The second shoe made a more satisfying sound, connecting with nasal cartilage. The snoring came to an abrupt halt, and Mike was finally able to drift off to sleep.

In the morning, Mike woke and staggered out of bed toward the bathroom. He stopped when he saw me approaching from the other direction. "You were snoring like a maniac," he said.

"You heard me all the way from my room?"

"What are you talking about? You were sleeping in the other bed. Next to mine."

"Not me," I said. "That was Father Carey."

Mike turned pale. "Don't worry," I reassured him. "He probably won't remember. He had a few sherries himself."

||||||||||||||||||||||||||||||||||||||||||||||||||||||||||||||||||||||||||||||||||||||||||||||||||||||||||||||||||||||||||||||||||||||||||

In the Middle Ages, Church officials would occasionally blame bad batches of beer on witchcraft. The last known burning at the stake of a beer witch is reported to have taken place in 1591.

||||||||||||||||||||||||||||||||||||||||||||||||||||||||||||||||||||||||||||||||||||||||||||||||||||||||||||||||||||||||||||||||||||||||||

REHAB

"Why is it that when you drink seven nights a
week in college you're a partyer, but after that
you're an alcoholic?"
—Anonymous

 Nowadays when we hear the word "passion," we tend to think of something good or exciting. We're encouraged to live with passion, to be passionate about our work and favorite sports teams, and to bring passion into the bedroom.

Passion has come a long way. The word was originally used to mean "suffering," specifically the kind of thorny-crowned, nails-in-the-palms suffering endured by Jesus Christ. (These are the kinds of things a lifetime of Catholic education will teach you.) In other words, passion is pain.

I've been lucky in that my passion for beer has done me more good (a family, a career, thousands and thousands of happy moments) than harm (weight gain, the fact that I would probably die of a heart attack if I ever sat down and pored over my lifetime bar tab). I know that not everyone is so lucky. I've got plenty of friends and family in recovery. Sometimes I've even helped get them there. I mean I've *literally* helped get them there.

In the late 1980s, I had one relative whose drinking got so bad that we arranged for him to check into Hazelden, the famous rehabilitation clinic in Minnesota. This relative—whom we'll call "Al" for the purposes of our story—wasn't in any shape to get there on his own. Somehow it was decided that my cousin Kelly and I would pick him up and drive him to the clinic, which was several hundred miles away from where we were collecting Al.

Al was drunk when we picked him up, which made it a whole lot easier to get him into the backseat of Kelly's car. But his buzz wore off a few minutes into the trip. A few hours into the drive, Al was trembling with the shakes.

"What should we do?" Kelly asked.

"I dunno," I replied. "Maybe get him a beer?"

I know, it wasn't exactly a responsible suggestion, but we still had hours to go until we reached Hazelden. Kelly and I weren't ready to deal with a full-on meltdown in the backseat, which seemed to be where Al was headed. And besides, we'd be making up for any harm we did him in the short run by getting him into rehab. So we pulled into the next gas station we passed and bought him a six-pack.

The plan worked—Al settled back into a happy stupor. The drive continued peacefully through the night until we reached the Mississippi River, when Kelly noticed flashing lights in his rearview mirror.

"The cops!" he said.

"What did you do?" I asked.

"Nothing!" Kelly insisted. "I was going like two miles an hour over the speed limit."

As soon as we were over the bridge, Kelly pulled over to the side of the road. Two policemen approached Kelly's side of the car. He rolled down his window.

"Do you know how fast you were going?" asked the younger of the two cops.

"I thought I was going the speed limit," Kelly replied.

"You were actually going a little faster than that," the cop answered, his tone bordering on arrogance.

The older cop stepped in. "Sorry about that," he said. "We're actually doing a training exercise. Don't worry, we're not really going to ding you for . . . do I smell *beer*?"

The cops shined their flashlights on Al, who was happily sipping from one of the cans. Or as a judge might call it, an "open container." The older officer ordered Kelly to step out of the car. We told the officers the truth—that we were taking Al to Hazelden—and after taking us through a few sobriety tests and a lot of questions, they decided to buy our story and sent us on our way.

It was after midnight when we finally pulled up to Hazelden. Kelly, who'd driven the whole way, looked like shit. We were both haggard and exhausted. Only Al, who had worked through the last of his six-pack, had a smile on his face. The facility's main office was closed, but there was a doorbell, so we rang and waited, hoping that we weren't going to have to find an all-night liquor store for another sixer to help get Al through the night.

A couple of minutes later, a nurse opened the front door to let us in. Her eyes swept over all three of us, settling on me. Not only was I the largest target but also the most recognizable—a television celebrity known for sitting on a barstool. She gave me her best Nurse Ratched smile.

"So, are we ready?"

It took me a couple of seconds to put two and two together. "Me? No, not me."

"Are you sure?" she asked.

"I'm sure."

"I see." The nurse turned toward Kelly, his eyes bloodshot from caffeine and late-night driving. "So are WE ready?"

We finally convinced her that Al was the one who needed help. Having done our job, Kelly and I climbed back into the car and drove all the way to Chicago, careful not to break the speed limit.

The Ultimate Health Food

A couple of times a year I travel down to Torrance, California, for a checkup at the Harbor-UCLA Medical Center. The
visits are almost always the same: They tell me that I need to
take better care of myself, especially when it comes to my
diet.

I love these little sojourns, not because of any fondness
for doctors, but because the hospital is close to Alpine Village,
a self-proclaimed "Little Village of the Alps" in the middle of
Southern California. The place is like a miniature Bavarian
hamlet, where I can stock up on sausages and German beers
that are almost impossible to find anyplace else.

If that sounds to you like I'm contravening my doctor's

orders, you're only half right. While I could probably live without the sausages, the beer might be what's keeping me alive.

Consider the facts:

1. Beer fights cancer. The hops used to make beer are loaded with polyphenols, chemicals that some scientists believe can slow the growth of human cancer cells.

2. Beer fights heart disease. Over sixty studies have shown that beer lovers enjoy many of the same positive effects as the people who swear by red wine. And it's been proven that moderate drinkers of any alcohol are up to a third less likely to die of a heart attack.

3. Beer makes you smarter. "Well ya see, Norm," begins one of my favorite monologues from *Cheers*, delivered by John "Cliff Clavin" Ratzenberger, "It's like this. . . . A herd of buffalo can only move as fast as the slowest buffalo. . . ." Alcohol, Cliff goes on to explain, does for the human brain what natural selection does for the herd—killing off the weakest cells, allowing the brain to function more efficiently. "That's why you always feel smarter after a few beers," he concludes.

A funny speech, only you can forget about what you've heard about beer killing brain cells. Several studies have shown that moderate drinking can help reduce age-related mental decline, and might even *improve* memory, reasoning, and problem solving.

4. Beer is the original Vitamin Water. Beer doesn't just start with a "B"—it's also loaded with B-vitamins, especially niacin (B_3), pantothenic acid (B_5), pyridoxine (B_6), and folate (B_9), plus smaller amounts of thiamin (B_1), riboflavin (B_2), and a couple of varieties of vitamin B_{12}.

5. Beer is good for your kidneys. While drinking gets a bad rap on account of the potential for liver damage, studies have shown that it may reduce the chances of kidney stones by up to 40 percent.

6. Beer is a stress buster. For most people, beer offers a chance to relax, socialize with friends, and have a few laughs. Given what we've learned about the relationship between a positive outlook on life and good health, it's hardly shocking that moderate drinkers, on the whole, report better health than teetotalers.

Egyptologists studying ancient texts have discovered several hundred medical prescriptions that required the use of beer.

GROWN-UP BEHAVIOR

"We old folks have to find our cushions
and pillows in our tankards.
Strong beer is the milk of the old."
—Martin Luther

 Bernadette's brother Joe is a career prosecutor who at times has sought higher office. He's a Republican, which we try not to hold against him, as (1) he's pretty liberal on social issues; and (2) it's not like the Democratic party is always so great. After all, when Joe lost his bid for lieutenant governor of Illinois in 2006, the winning ticket was headlined by a guy named Rod Blagojevich.

Plus he's family, which is why, back in 2002, Bernadette and I agreed to perform in a fundraiser for his run for Illinois Attorney General. John Ratzenberger joined me onstage for a Norm/Cliff reunion. We also pulled together some of the old Second City guys—including Tim Kazurinsky, Pete Burns, and Danny Breen—to do a few skits with Bernadette and me.

Our dear friend Joyce Sloane, a veteran producer of Second City, came to see us perform. Afterward she told us how refreshing it was to see good, smart political humor, then asked if we had any interest in going to Vienna. It turned out that for the last ten years or so Joyce had been booking a Second City touring company for a two-week-long gig in an English-language theater in Vienna, Austria. She wondered if we'd be interested in reconstituting our act and going on the road.

Despite being a sucker for her flattery, I was pretty sure what she really wanted out of us was maturity—the Austrians are a pretty strait laced crowd, and some of the younger comedians she'd booked in the past hadn't exactly kept to the straight and narrow. A group of Second City graybeards was just the ticket. By our age, we had grown to be thoughtful, mature, and, most of all, well behaved. Or so she thought.

Whatever maturity she was counting on started to disappear during a long delay at the airport, where Danny stumbled across a gift shop that sold novelty items, namely fake vomit and dog poop. Demonstrating the kind of restraint that only comes with age, Danny held off sharing his discovery until we reached Vienna. Specifically, until we reached the stage in Vienna. In the middle of our act, he placed the fake poop on a chair just before Tim Kazurinsky sat down. Tim was livid. The rest of us thought it was hilarious.

The poop quickly became a running joke, one that Danny insisted was a bedrock institution in the theater world. ("Since the days of the great John Barrymore," he claimed.) We named the gag after a store we passed every morning on the way to the theater, which housed a specialist in doll repair, or what in German you would call a *Puppendoktor*. "Courtesy of *der Poopin' Doctor!*" we'd scream, every time someone sat down in a pile of fake shit. Lame? Sure. Childish? Of course. But so fucking funny.

It might have been fine if we'd stopped there. Unfortunately, our training demanded ever greater heights of spontaneity. One night, after way too many beers, Tim suggested that we replace the plastic poop with the real thing. Pete Burns recovered a fresh pile in a nearby park. When Danny Breen woke the next morning, he found a plastic sack of dog shit hanging from his door.

Danny wanted payback, but he was already late for our matinee show. He dropped the sack in the sink in his bathroom—revenge would have to wait until later—and staggered off to the theater. When Danny got back to the hotel, the manager was waiting for him.

"Meester Breen?" the manager asked as Danny walked through the lobby. Maybe it was just me, but a lot of Austrians had accents that made them sound more like Nazis than the Nazis probably did.

"That's me," Danny helpfully replied. He shouldn't have—the manager was holding up a small but very fragrant bag that had been recovered by a clearly horrified member of the housekeeping staff.

"Vat is dis?"

"Oh that? That's just a joke. . . ."

"NO, Meester Breen. Let me assure you that poo-poo is not a joke."

Danny did his best to explain. He pulled out the fake poop. He told the manager about the days of the great John Barrymore. "It's supposed to be funny!" he insisted.

"Dis is vat you tink is funny?" the manager replied. "Dat vomen have to remove your poop from die sink? Ve cannot have dis kind of behavior at our hotel! You must leave. Immediately."

Fortunately, Joyce Sloane was able to negotiate our re-admission to the hotel. We celebrated by drinking at a nearby bar.

WHEN IN AUSTRIA . . .

Years later I'm still scratching my head as to what could have caused us to behave so immaturely. The best answer I've heard is the simplest. "It's Austria, George," Tim Kazurinsky later pointed out to me. It's kind of a rigid country, which only brought out the rebellious inner child in each of us—and in Austria, beer is the way to let loose.

The average Austrian drinks nearly thirty gallons of beer each year. (Americans are only good for about twenty.) There are more breweries per capita there than in any country in the world. At Christmastime, they brew *Samiclaus*, a dark, spicy lager that's about three times as strong as a Bud. No wonder we behaved so badly.

Not to brag, but I never have "too much beer." No matter how much I drink, I can almost always keep it together. Except, for some reason, in Vienna. Once I'd polished off a few Austrian brews, my eyes went to half mast. I started to lean backward when I walked, my feet leading the way for the rest of my body—better for balance, and easier to see, buying me a little extra time to react to things like furniture, walls, and lampposts. I wasn't the only drunk among us— we all spent a lot of the week singing and carrying on. So much so, in fact, we were kicked out of a bar. For laughing.

"Your laughter, it is too loud!" the bar's owner told us.

"Excuse me?"

"NOTTING is that funny."

Clearly.

The Morning After

While I'm not complaining, it's never been exactly clear to me how alcohol gets a free pass in relation to other drugs. I mean, imagine you're watching a Coors commercial, and at the end some unseen narrator told you that drinking beer might have certain side effects, including headaches, dehydration, diarrhea, nausea, loss of appetite, fatigue, trouble sleeping, increased sensitivity to light and sound, or the desire to crawl into a hole and die.

Maybe we're just so used to hangovers that they no longer rate as anything but normal. Only recently have they been studied with any scientific precision: There wasn't even a scientific name for the phenomenon until about ten years ago, when two creative doctors dubbed it *veisalgia*, pairing *algia*—

the Greek word for "pain"—with *kveis*—a Norwegian word for "uneasiness following debauchery." (Begging the question: How great a language is Norwegian?)

I've always believed that the best way to avoid a hangover is the three A.M. sausage pizza. I was thus delighted to discover that science has proved me correct. Fatty foods line the stomach and slow down the absorption of alcohol—giving your body time to play catch-up—while the interplay between the protein-rich sausage and the carbohydrates in the crust replaces your body's vital amino acids.

Here are a few other hangover cures that actually work:

1. Drinking water and/or fruit juice
2. Eating eggs and bananas
3. Popping vitamins
4. Time

And here are a few old wives' tales that, contrary to popular belief, will actually leave you feeling worse:

1. Coffee (the caffeine will make you even more dehydrated)
2. Fried food (it keeps your body too busy digesting to break down the alcohol in your system)
3. Painkillers with acetaminophen (combined with alcohol, it's like putting your liver into the ring with Mike Tyson)
4. The breakfast beer (says science—I'm still not convinced)

II

Los Angeles has a rap as being a substandard drinking town: The bars close promptly at two A.M., and everyone drives everywhere, putting a natural limit on overconsumption. But the city more than makes up for its warts with its late-night, beer-friendly, hangover-reducing eating options. Where else are you going to find a burrito truck at four in the morning? Or walk out of a game to the sight (and smell) of a grill loaded with bacon-wrapped sausages?

IIIIIIIIIIIIIIIIIIIIIIIIIIIIIIIIIIIIIIIIIIIIIIIIIIIIIIIIIIIIIIIIIIIIIIIIIIIIIIIIIIIIIIIIIIIIIIIIIIIIIIIIIIIIIIIIIIIIIIIIIIIIIIIIIIIIIIIIIIIIIIIIIIIIIIIIIIIIIIII

ON
CELEBRITY

"I wish that being famous helped prevent
me from being constipated."
—Marvin Gaye

 I was once sitting in a bar in Seattle when I noticed a guy staring at me. It kind of goes with the territory when you spend eleven seasons on a hit TV show, but it's not something that you ever really get used to.

Anyway, after staring at me for ten or fifteen minutes, the guy decided to approach me. "You know," he began, "you look an awful lot like that guy from *Cheers*."

"Yeah, I get that sometimes," I replied.

The guy leaned closer. "Listen . . ." he said. "I have a friend, an agent who reps celebrity lookalikes. You know, for meetings and parties and stuff. I bet he could find you some work."

I toasted him with my beer glass. "Thanks, but not interested."

"Whatever," he muttered, returning to his end of the bar. A few minutes later, he was back again. "Seriously, it's easy money. You just show up at a conference or something and you can make a couple hundred dollars a pop."

"Like I said, I appreciate the offer. But not interested."

"You got something against money?"

The guy went on to hector me for nearly a half hour, letting me know in no uncertain terms just how dumb I was for turning down his offer. I just put on my best dumb smile and let him go.

Sometimes I get mistaken for other famous people. I can't tell you how many times I've tried to settle my bill only to have a bartender tell me "It's on the house, Mr. Goodman. Loved your work on *Roseanne*." When I finally met John Goodman, I gushed to him over how much goodwill and free beer he'd racked up over the last twenty years. Goodman laughed, admitting that he'd probably scored twice that amount from people who had mistaken him for me.

A lot of times I'll get half recognized. When I travel through Dublin, for example, I'll hear people behind me murmuring "Jesusgodalmighty, it's fucking whatchamacallit! Your man! Go take a look!"

The times people do recognize me mostly result in good experiences. I'm often treated, as my wife, Bernadette, likes to observe, as life's guest. Free beer is only part of the story—I also get a lot more attention from the ladies than any fat man should, from feisty seniors to tramp-stamped girls my daughter's age. Needless to say, Bernadette isn't so pleased to have a chick-magnet for a husband. A particularly uncomfortable moment in our marriage occurred at a party in Boston celebrating the 200th episode of *Cheers*, when an attractive woman who worked for a local beer distributor, seemingly oblivious to Bernadette beside me, walked up to me and said, "I've always wanted to do this." The "this" turned out to be flashing her breasts. At another party, a gorgeous bartender just plopped herself on my lap. "Excuse me," said Bernadette, who was sitting right across from me. "Are you lost?"

"No . . ."

"Yes you are," my wife insisted, giving an icy stare to the now-terrified bartender, who quickly scurried away.

Fortunately for me, I'm nice to *any* well-wishers who say hello. So if Bernadette starts to get upset when I'm talking to a knockout beauty, I can deflect her with logic. "What, you want me to discriminate against the hot chicks?"

I don't mean to sound like I'm some kind of stud with the ladies, because I'm not—except for Bernadette, who remains a stunning beauty to this day. Someone once asked me the secret to a successful thirty-year marriage. "Having a big dick helps," I admitted. "Fortunately, Bernadette is very gentle with me."

Just because you are a celebrity doesn't mean that you're not affected by celebrity. In the late 1980s I did a play called

Super Sunday at the Williamstown Theatre Festival in Massachusetts. My costar, Jimmy Naughton, was a close friend of the great Paul Newman, and one night Newman came to cheer Jimmy on. Afterward, they invited me to go out drinking with them. I was star-struck the entire time, as in "Holy fuck, I'm drinking beer with Paul Newman!" I was all ears—the only time I opened my mouth was to pour beer into it. The best part of the night was when the waitress announced last call. Newman frowned, looked at his watch, strode to the bar, and returned with eighteen bottles of Beck's on a cocktail tray. "Waitress doesn't think we can finish these by closing time . . ." he said to me. Over the course of the next half hour, we proved her wrong.

Sometimes celebrity is just weird. I was lucky enough to appear in a couple of movies with the late Farrah Fawcett, who to me will always be the (Charlie's) Angel in the red bathing suit, the smiling girl in a poster you could once find hanging in nearly every college dormitory in the world. When my friend Pete Goldfinger heard I was working with Farrah on a project, he got down on his hands and knees. "I'm planning my brother's bachelor party. He *loves* Farrah. Maybe you could get him something from her."

"What, like an autograph?"

"No, like her underwear."

"I don't think Farrah wears a bra," I whispered.

Pete just smiled. "Believe me, we all know."

"So that means . . ."

Pete nodded. "Preferably unlaundered," he added.

Let it never be said that I'm not a good friend. I went ahead and shared the request with Farrah. Sure, it was a little embarrassing, but I figured, what the hell? Farrah was a great sport: After a long day of shooting, she had the film's costume department send over the thong she'd worn, barely the size of the postage stamp I used to send it to Pete.

I forgot all about the transaction until I ran into Pete again a few months later. I asked him what he'd done with the thong. "Let's just say there was a teakettle involved." Pete grinned. "The taste was brisk. Refreshing."

"Jesus!" I yelled. "Enough information, thanks."

But, hands down, the best part of being a celebrity? I get asked to do a lot of beer commercials.

There's an old story about Tom Erhart, a well-regarded Chicago actor who used to be the voice of Schlitz beer. This was a prime gig in the 1970s, a cushy job that Tom probably enjoyed. Until the day he walked into a bar and was greeted by the bartender: "Hello, Mr. Erhart. I guess you'll be having a Schlitz."

"Are you kidding me?" Erhart snapped back, adding (according to local legend), "I don't drink that piss." Unfortunately, this exchange took place in a bar that happened to be popular with journalists. Erhart's quote showed up in the next day's paper, and his career as Schlitz spokesman was over.

I've never had to worry about making that kind of mistake. I've done ads for Stroh's, Meisterbrau, Coors Light, Tuborg, Smithwick's, and Molson, and I happily enjoy drinking all of them. When I did an ad for Miller, the company was so concerned about adhering to the FTC's truth-in-advertising laws that they kept me swimming in the stuff for years. More regular than my newspaper or water delivery professional, the Miller Man showed up every month without fail, carrying two cases of beer into my house.

My favorite beer commercial was one I did by accident. In the late '80s, I was hired to play a villain in an action thriller shot in New Zealand called *Never Say Die*. Hoping to get into character, I used the plane trip to introduce myself to Steinlager, New Zealand's most popular beer.

Several Steinlagers later—or sixteen hours in real time— the plane landed in Auckland. I was jet-lagged, I'd crossed the International Date Line, and when I flushed the toilet, water spiraled the wrong way down the drain. All I wanted to do was to take a nap. But on the way to my hotel from the airport, someone asked me if I'd mind making a quick stop at the cricket stadium. There was some huge match going on—the cricket equivalent of the World Series—and the movie's producers wanted me to sit in with the commentators for whatever the cricket equivalent of an inning was. It was a rare opportunity to promote a picture before a frame was even shot.

So instead of napping, I found myself chatting with two cheery New Zealanders about a game I know nothing about. I was relieved when the conversation turned to beer. "So, Jawge," one of them said, "have ya had a chance to try any of ah New Zealand behs?"

"I sure did," I answered. "Had a few of those Steinlagers on the plane over. Good stuff."

The chatter came to an immediate halt, replaced by dead air. The announcers stared back at me like I'd just insulted the Queen. "You guys don't like Steinlager?"

"Uh Jawge, this is state TV. Weh not allowed to do any commehcial advehtising."

Oops. A few hours into the country and I'd already gotten in trouble. Fortunately the interview concluded without any further international incidents and I got back to my hotel room in time for a before-dinner nap.

I slept like a king until I was woken by the sound of an alarm beeping. Only when I reached over to turn off the clock, there wasn't one to be found. There was, however, a truck backing up to the hotel, several floors below my window. A few minutes later, a gentleman in a Steinlager jumpsuit appeared at my door with a handtruck. He began to unload Steinlager hats, mugs, luggage, jackets, a Steinlager director's chair with my name stitched into it, and, of course, many cases of Steinlager beer. He gave me a handwritten note from the brewmaster thanking me for my help and inviting me for a personal tour, which I happily accepted. I was still sweating Steinlager when I got back to the States.

DRINKING WITH WOODY

WOODY

Can I pour you a beer, Mr. Peterson?

NORM

A little early, isn't it, Woody?

WOODY

For a beer?

NORM

No, for stupid questions.

 From the outside, it might seem like the casts of successful television shows all get along, and the great group chemistry creates a better show. That's partially true. The other part of the equation is that when a show is actually good, everyone is so excited that the chemistry follows. But I think ev-

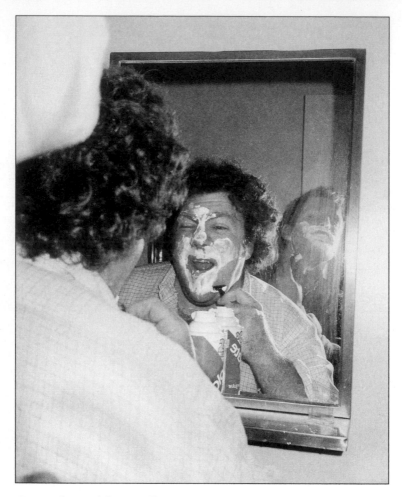

Grooming with Woody.

eryone on *Cheers* felt an instant connection to Woody Harrelson, who joined the show after we lost "Coach" Nicholas Colasanto to a heart attack near the end of our third season. While the real-life Woody is a lot shrewder than the character he played on the show, the fictional Woody's expansive personality and generous spirit aren't part of any act.

When *Cheers* ended, we had a wrap party in an airplane hangar at Santa Monica Airport. There was live music—Los Lobos!—and someone handed out giant Cohiba cigars. If you've ever smoked a Cohiba, you know it's a serious piece of tobacco engineering. Smoked properly, it's one of the most incredible sensory experiences known to man. In the wrong hands, it's a one-way ticket to misery. Or at least intense nausea and dizziness, which is what I was feeling after a few puffs. I've never been much of a cigar smoker.

By the time the party ended, I was lying on the floor. I must have looked green, because Woody—who's never met a green cause he didn't like—offered me a trash bag. "Thanks," I said, and puked into the bag.

Woody started to say "You're welcome," but the sight (and smell) of the barf was too much. He grabbed the bag back from me just in time.

It's not easy to laugh and puke at the same time, but we managed. Bernadette, who didn't find the situation quite as funny as we did, arranged for the hangar doors to be opened so that a car could drive directly up to where I was still lying. I was shoveled into the backseat, and Bernadette rode shotgun with the driver.

Over the years, Woody and I have been invited to a few charity events together. One was in Cabo San Lucas, Mexico. Cabo is a just a couple of hours by plane from Los Angeles, but in terms of weather, it's a whole different world. When Woody and I landed, we discovered that we'd traded a warm, breezy September day in Los Angeles for harsh sun, temperatures in the hundreds, and humidity so thick you could practically see it.

MY FAVORITE MEXICAN BEERS

1. Bohemia

2. Pacifico

3. A tie: **Corona** and **Dos Equis.** I'm a sucker for good advertising. Corona has been nailing it for years—the commercials alone are enough to relax me—while Dos Equis has recently won my heart with their "World's Most Interesting Man" campaign.

A lot of people will tell you that if you have to put a lime into your beer to make it taste better, you're not drinking a good beer. To which I say: Bah! The Germans have been putting lemons into their *Weisbeer* for centuries.

We began sweating the second we stepped off the plane. Then the van that took us to the resort—an hour's drive from the airport—didn't have working air-conditioning. Two minutes into the drive, Woody turned to me and said,

"Buddy, as soon as I get to the hotel, I'm going to walk straight into the ocean."

"Uh-uh," I croaked. "Beers first, *then* we'll walk straight into the ocean."

"Even better."

When we got to the hotel, we found out we'd be sharing a private villa sitting right next to the ocean on a white sand beach. "I don't think I can wait for that beer," Woody said, already shedding clothes on his way toward the water.

"I'm right behind you." I stripped down to my shorts and waded into the ocean. Everything was right in the world—the water temperature, the view, the giant wave heading my way . . .

POW! The wave plowed into me. Spin. Slam. Repeat. The pummeling continued for a couple of minutes before I washed up on shore. When I shook my head, sand flew out of my eyes, ears, and hair. The world slowly began to come back into focus. "Hey, buddy!" I heard Woody yell. "I think I'm gonna catch a wave!" I looked at him just in time to see another mini-tsunami deliver a similar beating.

The wave eventually deposited Woody on the shore next to me. We staggered back to the villa. A very large sign next to the door—one we couldn't have missed had we entered the villa before going to the beach—was printed in big block letters: "DANGER!!! NO SWIMMING IN FRONT OF BUNGALOWS!"

"Guess we shouldn't have skipped the beer," I said. It

turns out we had inadvertently waded into some of the most notorious rough surf in the world. I stuck to drinking by the pool for the rest of the trip.

Another time we were both invited to an event in Maui. When we arrived at the hotel, we went straight for the poolside bar. "Bad timing," the bartender said. "You just missed the U.S. Women's Synchronized Swimming Team. They did a show in the pool."

Big whoop, we thought, until dinner, when a coterie of gorgeous women with Olympic bodies invaded the buffet line. "Wow," I managed.

Woody looked pained. "Man, I can't believe we missed the show."

I was too happily married and terrified of my wife to even think about straying, but Woody was, at the time, still a single guy. I couldn't help but feel sympathy.

"Wood, relax. I'll get them to do a show for us."

"How are you going to do that?"

"I don't know yet. But I will a few beers from now."

Some people claim that sex gets better as they get older. Those people are mostly full of shit. If there is an upside, it's that your expectations are diminished. You quit holding out for the complete package and learn to appreciate whatever's there. A great ass. Bright eyes. A friendly tone of voice. And in my case, a beautiful wife who will still put up with me after thirty years.

Several beers later, we'd forgotten all about the women. We finished dinner and moved to a bar on the beach. At around midnight, three or four of the swimmers walked into the bar. "Time for that plan of yours," Woody said.

"I'll improvise," I replied. I stumbled over to the swimmers' table and told them how disappointed we were to have missed their earlier show. Fortunately, the women recognized Woody and me from *Cheers*, which was apparently a good enough excuse for them to look past my crappy opening line. They invited us to join them.

We chatted for about twenty minutes before I turned the conversation back toward their show. "Too bad the pool's closed," one of the swimmers said. "We could have done a private show for you guys."

"Who needs a pool?" I said. "We've got the ocean! Not to mention moonlight, tiki torches, and beers on the beach." I could see their resistance starting to diminish.

"We'd have to put on our suits . . ." one of the other swimmers countered.

"You don't need swimsuits," I scoffed. "Swimsuits are for the pool—this is nature. This is how shows like yours have been performed in the South Sea Islands for centuries. Have you seen *Mutiny on the Bounty*? I'll tell you what, if it makes you feel more comfortable, Woody and I will take off our clothes too."

"You don't have to do that," one of the women quickly replied. "We'll get our suits. You'll like our suits. We'll be back in five minutes."

The swimmers left the bar. Ten minutes later, having given up any hope of their ever returning, I paid the tab and got up to go back to our bungalow. When I turned to Woody, he had a huge grin on his face. "What?" I asked.

"Look," he replied, pointing toward the ocean. The women, in swimsuits, were bounding toward the water to reprise their show. "I think we should join them."

And that is how Woody and I wound up performing with the U.S. Women's Olympic Synchronized Swimming Team. After the show, I went straight to bed. The last I saw of Woody that night, he was in the Jacuzzi with a few of the swimmers. It wasn't the first time I've left Woody in a Jacuzzi full of beautiful women; somehow I suspected it wouldn't be the last.

SUPERFANS

"Da Bears."

—Bob Swerski

 I'll be the first to admit that I lucked into the role of Norm Peterson, a character whom I'd been training to play my whole life. What I find even more amazing is that I've been struck by this kind of lightning more than once: Toward the end of *Cheers*, I was invited to play a guy from Chicago who lived for drinking beer, cheering for the Bears, and gorging himself on Polish sausages. Clearly, I didn't have to stretch much to play "Superfan" Bob Swerski.

If you've never seen any of the Superfan sketches, they involve a group of guys (and the occasional lady) with exaggerated Chicago accents who live in awe of "Da Bears," "Da Bulls," and former Bears coach Mike Ditka. Written by Robert Smigel, most of the bits aired on *Saturday Night Live*, but as the Swerski Brothers grew in popularity, we made appearances in TV specials and at Super Bowls. As recently as

Living the dream.

this year, Smigel and I donned the costumes for a fundraiser with the legendary Coach Ditka himself. But the truth is, it's not anywhere near as much fun without the late Chris Farley.

An original member of the Superfans, Chris Farley was one of the funniest people I've ever met. I struggled for years on the stage to find my comic voice; Chris joined Second City (and, later, *SNL*) with his voice already fully developed, a fact I've confirmed through conversations with my friend Pat Finn, who went to college with him.

While attending Marquette University, Pat and Chris signed up for a public-speaking class. The coursework wasn't a challenge for either of them—both were hilarious guys with a natural gift for improv—so they took it upon themselves to increase the level of difficulty. When asked to give impromptu speeches on what they did last summer, Pat shared his experiences as an air-conditioning repairman, while Chris expounded on life as a circus barker. Absolutely none of it was true.

One day Pat decided to up the ante by suggesting Chris drink a six-pack of tall boys. *During* class. Chris wasn't the kind of guy who needed a lot of prodding.

"Today we'll be giving extemporaneous speeches that tell us how to *do* something," the teacher began. "Who would like to—Mr. Farley, are you drinking beer in class?"

Chris burped. "Uh, yes?"

"I see," the teacher replied. "Then maybe you'd like to begin. Would you come up to the front of the room and teach us how to do something?"

"Sure," Chris replied. He walked up to the front of the room, but instead of stopping at the podium, he walked out into the hallway and closed the door behind him. For a few seconds, the class sat there in stunned silence. The silence was broken by a primal scream from the hallway. Then the door flew open, and Chris—his shirt pulled over his head to expose his belly—ran back into the classroom and in a single leap landed with both feet on top of the teacher's desk. Everybody stared at him in amazement—what was he going to do next?

He opened another sixteen-ounce can, chugged it in one gulp, winged it against the blackboard in the back of the room, and let out a mighty belch. "How to get someone's attention, by Chris Farley," he grumbled. "Thank you." Then he got down off the desk, returned to the back of the classroom, and opened another beer. The teacher might not have been happy, but what could he do? It wasn't like anyone in the class was going to do a more effective job with the assignment.

We miss you, Chris.

HOW TO SHOTGUN A BEER

1. Tilt can at 45-degree angle.

2. Using a key or small knife, punch a hole in the bottom of the can.

3. Place mouth over hole.

4. Open top of can. The beer will rush out of the bottom hole, hopefully into your mouth.

Bar Theory, Part Three

It doesn't matter who you are or where you're from—beer is about bringing people together. Here are seventy-seven different ways to say "Cheers!" no matter where you are.

Seventy-seven Toasts from Around the World

Afrikaans	*Gesondheid*
Albanian	*Shendeti tuaj / Gezuar!*
Arabic	*Shucram / Fee sihetak (Egyptian)*
Armenian	*Genatz*
Asturian	*Gayola*
Australian	Bottoms up!
Austrian	*Prost / Zum Wohl*
Azerbaijani	*Afiyœt oslun*

Basque	*Topa*
Belgian	*Op uw gezonheid*
Bengali	*Joy*
Bosnian	*Zivjeli*
Brazilian	*Tchim Tchim / Sauté / Viva*
Breton	*Yec'hed mat*
Bulgarian	*Nazdrave*
Catalan	*Salut*
Chinese	*Kong chien / Nien Nien ne / Gan Bei*
Cornish	*Yeghes da*
Costa Rican	*Pura Vida*
Creole	*Salud*
Croatian	*Zivjeli / U zdravlje*
Czech	*Na zdraví*
Danish	*Skal*
Dutch	*Proost*
Egyptian	*Fee sihetak*
Esperanto	*Sanon*
Estonian	*Teie terviseks*
Farsi	*Ba'sal'a'ma'ti*
Finnish	*Kippis*
French	*A votre santé*
Frisian	*Tsjoch*
Galician	*Chinchín / Saúde*
German	*Prost*
Greek	*Gia'sou / Eis igian*
Greenlandic	*Kasugta*
Hawaiian	*Hipahipa / Okole maluna*

Hebrew	*L'chaim*
Hindi	*Apki Lambi Umar Ke Liye*
Holooe	*Kam-poe*
Hungarian	*Egészségedre*
Icelandic	*Santanka nu / Skal*
Ido	*Ye vua saneso*
Irish Gaelic	*Slánte*
Italian	*Salute / Cin cin*
Japanese	*Kampai*
Korean	*Konbe*
Latin	*Sanitas bona / Bene tibi*
Latvian	*Prieka*
Lithuanian	*I sveikata*
Malaysian	*Minum*
Mandarin	*Gan bei*
Mexican	*Salud*
Moroccan	*Saha wa'afiab*
Norwegian	*Skal*
Occitan	*A la vòstra*
Pakistani	*Sanda bashi*
Philippine	*Mabuhay*
Polish	*Na zdrowie*
Portuguese	*Saúde*
Rumanian	*Noroc*
Russian	*Vashe zdorovie / Na zdrovia*
Serbian	*Zivjeli*
Sesotho	*Nqa*
Slovak	*Na zdravie*

Slovenian	*Na zdravje*
Spanish	*Salud*
Swahili	*Afya / Vifijo*
Swedish	*Skal*
Tagalog	*Mabuhay*
Thai	*Chook-die / Sawasdi / Chayoo / Che Loong*
Turkish	*Serefe*
Ukrainian	*Budmo*
Vietnamese	*Chia*
Welsh	*Lechyd da*
Yiddish	*L'chaim*
Yugoslavian	*Ziveo / Ziveli*
Zulu	*Oogy wawa*

BEER
AND FOOD

"Without question, the greatest invention
in the history of mankind is beer.
Oh, I grant you that the wheel was also
a fine invention, but the wheel does not
go nearly as well with pizza."
—Dave Barry

I am what you'd call a city mouse, born and raised in Chicago, living in Los Angeles, working frequently in Manhattan. I like gourmet coffee, air-conditioning, and supermarkets that sell seventeen different kinds of mustard. My only real taste of country living comes when I visit my wife Bernadette's family at their summer home in rural Michigan. It's the kind of place where the kids belong to 4-H and the adults have rules about roadkill—i.e., don't bother fussing with it when you pass it on the way into town. The new

corpses you see on the way home are the ones that are fresh enough to skin and eat.

Our visits to Michigan sometimes coincide with the Oceana County Fair, held at the end of every summer since the Civil War. Located in the town of Hart, the fair has everything a city mouse could hope for—pie-eating contests, heavyweight horsepulls, giant vegetables, homemade ceramics. And, of course, the opportunity to buy your own livestock.

It wasn't my idea to buy and roast a pig—that was Bernadette's brother Ray's brainchild—but it wasn't like I was going to say no. (What if it's good?) So when a barker announced the start of the livestock auction, Ray and I took seats in the front row, waited for a meaty sow to catch our eye, and started bidding.

We encountered competition. Specifically, a farmer, maybe fifty years old, wearing overalls. Every time we bid, he bid higher. "Guess you really want that pig," I said to him.

"Sure do," he replied. "My niece raised that pig from the time it was a baby."

Great, I thought. I'm bidding on Wilbur from *Charlotte's Web*. The little girl who raised the poor animal must be having second thoughts. I should let her uncle win. It would probably be the happiest moment of that little girl's life.

That's what I thought *to myself*. What I said out loud was, "One hundred dollars!"

"One twenty-five," the uncle replied.

It was the last weekend in August, so it was hot to begin with, but the auction tent started to feel a lot warmer. It could have been heat stroke, temporary madness, or just my competitive instincts, but with God as my witness, I was going to eat that pig.

The price kept going up and up. One fifty. Two hundred. Three hundred. I could hear the murmurs of astonishment rippling through the crowd. I mopped sweat from my brow by the towelful. The uncle bid three fifty—could this animal really be worth three hundred and fifty dollars? I looked to Ray for counsel. He just shrugged and threw up his hands.

It was time to fish or cut bait. "Five hundred dollars!" I yelled.

A hush fell over the tent. Everyone looked at the uncle, who seemed to be struggling with his decision. "Five hundred dollars," repeated the auctioneer. "Going once . . . going twice . . ." The uncle's hand started to rise, then dropped back down to his side. "Three times SOLD for five hundred dollars!"

People cheered. I shook the uncle's hand. The auctioneer told us we could pick up the pig in the pen. I probably should have felt ashamed for breaking a little girl's heart, but the truth was I was psyched to have won.

The pig was in the very back of the pen, which meant that to get her I would have to trudge through a pigshit swamp that came up to my ankles. I had no intention of doing this, so I sent my younger brother Tommy, causing him to ruin a new pair of penny loafers. Together we coaxed the animal into a horse-trailer and we drove a few miles to a farmer who would do the butchering. The killing was up to us. Well, not me exactly—this city mouse was too wimpy to kill his own food. Ray shot the pig in the temple with a hunting rifle.

The farmer who butchered the pig happened to have just picked a bushel basket full of new potatoes. "Those for sale?" I asked him.

He nodded. "Three seventy-five."

"This is turning out to be an expensive meal," I said, reaching for my wallet.

"Three *dollars*," the farmer corrected me. "And seventy-five cents."

"Here's a five. Keep the change."

Beer and food have this in common: They bring people together. We threw an old-time roast, and everyone—my family, my wife's family, the neighbors and their families—got to eat pig and drink beer late into the night.

PAIRING BEER AND FOOD

So what do you drink with a roasted pig? We drank cold American lager, which turned out to be a damn perfect complement to the juicy pork.

As beer has become more complicated—increasing its "snob appeal"—its connoisseurs have naturally spent a lot of time and ink trying to match their meals to the perfect brew. One general rule of thumb treats ales as red wines—complementing steaks, burgers, and other red meats—while lagers stand in for the whites, going well with chicken, seafood, and vegetable dishes. There are exceptions: corn-on-the-cob tastes great with a good ale; a lot of shellfish goes better with stout. And plenty of variations—dark porters play well with strong cheeses, while *Hefeweizen* may change the way you look at scrambled eggs.

But for me, it's less important to pair beer with food than with your environment. Give me a dark beer on a dark dreary day, and life is going to seem almost inexplicably brighter. Nothing's better than a frosty mug of yellow American lager at a hot summer picnic. Oktoberfest doesn't feel right without *Märzen*. There's nothing wrong with being a snob about what you eat and drink, but there's always so much more to a great meal than the flavor of the food.

A few months later, I got a letter from the little girl who raised the pig. I was afraid to open it, expecting tear-stained pages about how I'd mercilessly slaughtered her beloved Esmeralda. Instead I found a neatly written page containing a series of questions. "How was she? Did she taste good? Will you be back next year? I'm raising a lamb!"

Which is why at the next year's Oceana County Fair, I found myself in a bidding war for a baby sheep.

BEER NUTS

"Women. Can't live with them . . . pass the beer nuts."

—Norm Peterson

Further proof that beer is king: There's no such thing as a "wine cracker" or a "whiskey chip." But Beer Nuts have been around for years.

Like so many great things, Beer Nuts are from Illinois, where they began life as "Redskins." As some scholars have pointed out, this might be the only time in history that the name "Redskins" was used in a politically correct context—the peanuts were roasted and glazed with their red skins intact.

In the 1950s, a potato chip distributor convinced the manufacturer—the Shirk family of Bloomington, Illinois—to take advantage of a growing market for pub food. The "slightly sweet, lightly salted" snack was renamed "Beer Nuts," and business quickly began to boom. By the 1970s, the Shirks were producing ten million pounds of nuts a year.

Beer
or Bread?

While beer may be the most important stuff made out of grains, water, and yeast, it's not the only stuff. You smart kids out there can raise your hand if you knew that those same ingredients can be found in bread. You may also know (from reading this book) that the invention of bread was a pretty big deal at the time, transforming humanity from gnarling packs of hunter-gatherers into more refined communities of seed collectors and bakers. One popular explanation for the discovery of beer is that it arose from the dust of the brand-new breadmaking business.

Not so, says Dr. Solomon H. Katz, an Ivy League professor who studies ancient man.

If beer lovers have a favorite anthropologist, it would have to be Dr. Katz: He once helped San Francisco's Anchor Steam Brewery with their Sumerian Beer Project, the goal of which was to craft a beer as faithfully as possible to the recipes used by the first human beer-makers. But Dr. Katz's greatest achievement might be flipping the script on the relationship between bread and beer: It wasn't bakers who discovered brewing, theorizes Dr. Katz. It was the beer that begat the bread.

Archaeologists who study Neolithic villages have found all kinds of primitive tools used to cultivate grain. Dr. Katz is more interested in what hasn't been found: a lot of carbonized seeds. If the ancient villagers had been using that grain to cook bread, some of the grains would inevitably have burned and left traces of carbon. And some did, just not as many as the scientists might have expected. According to the Good Doctor, that's because a lot of these villagers weren't cooking these grains, they were fermenting them to make beer. The discovery of narrow-necked bottles perfect for storing beer—the original longnecks!—supports his theory that ancient brewers were the ones who started stockpiling seeds.

It's not too hard to connect the rest of the dots: Beer gets you drunk, being drunk makes you lazy, and when you're lazy you start to experiment with questions like "I wonder what happens if we cook it?" and "Maybe if we give some to the animals, we won't have to chase them when it's time to slaughter them." These original beer-loving slackers may very well have been the inventors of modern civilization as we know it.

LIKE THE ONRUSH OF THE
TIGRIS AND EUPHRATES

Argue all you want about which came first—the bread or the beer—but there's no getting around the fact that brewers have been around for as long as there have been civilizations. The ancient Sumerians, for example, didn't just love beer; they actually worshipped Ninkasi, a goddess whose primary job seemed to be watching over the brewing process. In the early 1990s, Dr. Solomon Katz teamed up with the Anchor Brewing Company to use a hymn to this goddess—one that predates Jesus by a couple of thousand years—to reproduce Sumerian beer. If you're an adventurous home brewer, you might try the same, although I have absolutely no clue where to find "bappir":

Borne of the flowing water, tenderly cared for by the Ninhursag.
Borne of the flowing water, tenderly cared for by the Ninhursag.

Having founded your town by the sacred lake, she finished its
*   great walls for you,*
Ninkasi, having founded your town by the sacred lake, she finished
*   its walls for you.*

Your father is Enki, Lord Nidimmud; your mother is Ninti, the queen
*   of the sacred lake.*
Ninkasi, your father is Enki, Lord Nidimmud; your mother is Ninti,
*   the queen of the sacred lake.*

You are the one who handles the dough [and] with a big shovel, mixing in a pit, the bappir with sweet aromatics.
Ninkasi, you are the one who handles the dough [and] with a big shovel, mixing in a pit, the bappir with date-honey.

You are the one who bakes the bappir in the big oven, puts in order the piles of hulled grains.
Ninkasi, you are the one who bakes the bappir in the big oven, puts in order the piles of hulled grains.

You are the one who waters the malt set on the ground; the noble dogs keep away even the potentates.
Ninkasi, you are the one who waters the malt set on the ground; the noble dogs keep away even the potentates,

You are the one who soaks the malt in a jar; the waves rise, the waves fall.
Ninkasi, you are the one who soaks the malt in a jar; the waves rise, the waves fall.

You are the one who spreads the cooked mash on large reed mats; coolness overcomes.
Ninkasi, you are the one who spreads the cooked mash on large reed mats; coolness overcomes.

You are the one who holds with both hands the great sweet wort, brewing it with honey and wine.

You the sweet wort to the vessel; Ninkasi, you the sweet wort to the vessel.

The filtering vat, which makes a pleasant sound, you place appropriately on a large collector vat.
Ninkasi, the filtering vat, which makes a pleasant sound, you place appropriately on a large collector vat.

When you pour out the filtered beer of the collector vat, it is like the onrush of Tigris and Euphrates.

Ninkasi, you are the one who pours out the filtered beer of the collector vat.

It is like the onrush of Tigris and Euphrates.

PARTY ANIMALS

"All animals are equal, but some animals are
more equal than others."
—George Orwell

There are plenty of stories in the Bible that don't make sense, but the one that used to bug me the most was Noah's Ark. It's one thing to squeeze that many animals aboard a ship, but feeding them all? It wasn't like Noah could just pull his boat into the nearest Petco.

A couple of years ago, I finally heard an explanation for this conundrum that made sense: some Biblical scholars believe that Noah might have stockpiled beer aboard the Ark. A few dozen kegs would have gone a long way toward keeping the animals happy.

• • •

Take our family dog Plato, for example.

My friend Pat, who knows me so well, once surprised me with a giant Pilsner Urquell–branded handle for my home keg. It would have been a perfect addition to my beer-drinking life if it hadn't been a little too top-heavy: a strong gust of wind could blow the tap open. I like to think it was a fly landing on the handle, in the middle of the night, who bore responsibility for spilling the contents of an entire keg of Pilsner Urquell onto my patio, but whatever it was, the result was as messy as it was hilarious.

You see, it wasn't me who discovered the accident, but Plato, our Jack Russell terrier. Maybe it was his British blood that led him to drink it all. Not like I was complaining—while the dog was drunk for days afterward, at least I didn't have to clean up the spilled beer. The only apparent downside was that Plato, from that day on, became a beer snob. We tried to wean him to more cost effective American lager, but he'd already had a taste of the good stuff, and there was no going back.

Even if he hadn't been a beer lover, Plato still would have led a legendary life. He was buff, like Superdog, and loved to chase squirrels up trees. When the squirrels began leaping a death-defying distance from the tree to the roof in order to escape him, my son Josh built an elaborate network of overlapping planks to bridge the gap, allowing Plato to vertically expand the range of his sentry duties. I'd occasionally get puzzled looks from the mailman. "You know you have a dog on your roof, right?" he'd ask.

"Just doing his job," I'd reply.

But his most amazing trick involved the swimming pool. My sons Josh and Andy figured out that Plato loved lemons almost as much as beer, so they would lock him behind a gate and tease him with the sour fruit, working him into a frenzy. Then they would place the lemon on a boogie board in the middle of our swimming pool and open the gate. Plato would come charging out like a bull, leaping from the edge of the pool onto the boogie board. His momentum would allow him to surf the board to the other side. Rad, dude!

Plato lived to a fine old age—fourteen—but grew increasingly bad-tempered toward the end of his life. Bernadette liked to compare him to Ben Kingsley in *Sexy Beast*, as his barks sounded less like "Woof! Woof! Woof!" and more like "Fuck! Fuck! Fuck!" In his final days, he lost his eyesight. But he never lost his taste for beer. As I move grudgingly into my golden years, I find myself taking a lot of comfort in that fact.

Dogs aren't the animal kingdom's only beer-lovers. Charles Darwin observed in *The Descent of Man* (a great name for a beer book, if T.C. Boyle hadn't already used it) that African tribesmen used beer as a lure to catch wild baboons. Some zookeepers serve up empty kegs as treats for their bears, who go wild for the smell. A species of Malaysian tree shrew has developed a symbiotic relationship with the bertam palm flower, a plant whose nectar naturally ferments into a kind of beer. I don't know what's more amazing: that there's a plant that brews its own beer, or that the tree shrew—a squirrel-sized critter whose love for the stuff helps to pollinate the plant—can polish off the equivalent of two six-packs in about two hours.

BEER AND . . . BUGS?

One summer my garden was overrun by slugs. Bernadette and I asked a gardener how to keep the slugs from devouring all of our plants, and the clever man—perhaps knowing what sort of tools we might have readily at our disposal—suggested that we fill a pie tin with beer.

Huh?

It turns out that slugs find the taste of beer absolutely irresistible, so much so that they'll drown themselves chasing it. Sure enough, the morning after we tried it, the pie tin was filled with floating slug carcasses. Slugs love beer, which, if you think about it, kind of makes sense.

Beer and the Limits of Human Endurance

In the early 1990s, the publishers behind *The Guinness Book of World Records* decided that for safety's sake, they'd no longer accept records related to beer consumption. This was good news for a Pennsylvania man named Steven Petrosino, as it ensured that his world-record chug—a liter of beer in just 1.3 seconds—was good for the ages. Here are a few more beer-related feats:

■ No one is sure about the record for the number of beers consumed, but many believe that the late wrestler Andre the

Giant—who reportedly drank 119 beers during a six-hour stretch—has it clinched.

■ The record for the fastest "Beer Mile"—a surprisingly popular athletic endeavor that involves drinking an entire beer before each of four laps around a quarter-mile track—belongs to a Canadian named Jim Finlayson. His time of 5 minutes, 9 seconds would be impressive even if he had been sober.

■ The citizens of the Czech Republic drink the most beer per person—nearly 160 liters each year—but no one can beat the United States in terms of raw volume: Americans down about 6.5 million gallons of beer every year.

LAST CALL

I'd Like A Great Lake Of Beer For The King Of
Kings/I Would Like To Be Watching Heaven's
Family Drinking It Through All Eternity.
—St. Brigid's Prayer

Like I said at the beginning of this book, I am a simple man.
Life, on the other hand, gets complicated, and beer, for its
many virtues, sometimes adds to the complexity. Drinking
unleashes the reins in ways that can be unpredictable, both
good and bad.

I don't want to make light work of the bad. I'm not 100%
proud of the things I've done while under the influence. I've
seen the love of drink rain hell on the lives of people that I
care about deeply.

But all in all, beer's been a boon companion on my life's
journey. It's helped to bring me closer to my family, from
grandparents to kids to in-laws. I've met new friends and
learned to better appreciate the old ones. As I've changed—

dare I say evolved?—beer has always kept pace: what began (for me) as a pale American lager has matured into a rich pastiche of unexpected flavors, colors, and aromas.

The adventure's not over yet. There are more brewers than ever combining the age-old methods, developed over thousands of years of human history, with all of kinds of modern innovations. The California coastline is dotted with craft breweries I haven't yet visited. I want to do my own version of the movie *Sideways*, starting in San Diego with Alesmith or the Stone Brewing Company, working my way north to "Beervana"—Portland, Oregon—the city with the highest concentration of breweries in the world. Or how about a boat ride up the river Scheldt, searching out obscure Belgian monasteries that have had hundreds of years to tinker with a recipe that was already pretty close to perfection? I can imagine myself turning into a sort of boozy Colonel Kurtz, lost not in a heart of darkness but in a haze of great brews. I want to have a beer in outer space, sipping a cold one with an astronaut's view of the planet Earth, content with the knowledge that no matter how advanced technology becomes, people are still going to be brewing beer in a way that an ancient Mesopotamian would have recognized. Whatever unforeseen future marvels and disasters await the human race, we're always going to have beer to help us make sense of them.

Thank you, beer. Damn glad to have met you.

ACKNOWLEDGMENTS

Thanks first and foremost to Jonathan Grotenstein for help-ing me to pull my thoughts together into what I hope has been an entertaining read.

We couldn't have done it, however, without a lot of help from my friends and family, so generous in their recollec-tions and photographs—especially the ones I've tried to for-get. The list begins with my mother, Loret Wendt, and my sister Kathy, my cousin and lifelong friend Kelly McCarthy, and a group of the finest drinking companions a man could hope for: Mike Begley, Danny Breen, Joe and Margaret Farmar, Pat Finn, Pete Goldfinger, Tim Kazurinsky, Joe and Sally Keenan, Mike McDonald, Dick Rolston, and Robert Smigel.

You probably wouldn't be reading this book if there had never been a Norm Peterson—thanks to Glen Charles, Les Charles, and Jimmy Burrows for having the brilliance to cre-ate a role that allowed me to take sitting on a barstool to a professional level. I'm also grateful to Joyce Sloane and everyone at Second City who transformed my natural goofiness into an actual trade.

Thank you, Woody Harrelson, not only for being a friend, but for allowing me to throw you under the proverbial bus. And to Chris Farley, who probably would have jumped in front of the bus himself if only he were still with us.

Thanks to my manager Geoff Cheddy and agent Dan Strone, who helped put this book together with Tricia Boczkowski, Emily Westlake, and the rest of the stellar crew at Simon Spotlight Entertainment. It's been an absolute pleasure working with all of you.

Finally, I owe my deepest gratitude to my beautiful wife, whose incredible assistance on the book was just another day at the office for a woman who has been keeping me going through thirty years of marriage. I love you, Bernadette.

ABOUT THE AUTHOR

George Wendt lives with his family in Southern California. He likes beer. A lot.